CHICKPEA COOKBOOK

100 Delicious and Nutritious Recipes to Elevate Your Cooking with Chickpeas

Cynthia Mitchell

Copyright Material ©2023

All Rights Reserved

No part of this book may be used or transmitted in any form or by any means without the proper written consent of the publisher and copyright owner, except for brief quotations used in a review. This book should not be considered a substitute for medical, legal, or other professional advice.

TABLE OF CONTENTS

TABLE OF CONTENTS..3
INTRODUCTION..7
BREAKFAST..8
1. Chickpea Crepe Tacos with Veal and Eggplant..............9
2. Pane di Ceci...12
3. Mushrooms Chickpea Crêpes...14
4. Chickpea Flour Crêpes...16
5. Chickpea Milk..18
6. Wheat & Meat Porridge...20
SNACKS..23
7. Roasted Chickpeas with aquafaba................................24
8. Quinoa stuffed onions...26
9. Pakora..28
10. Chickpea fritters with couscous..................................30
11. Chickpea Blinis with Mustard Micros.........................32
12. Chickpea Salad Crostini...35
13. Panisse bruschetta with Basil Microgreens................37
14. Chickpea Salad Pinwheels...40
15. Spiced chilli chickpeas...42
16. Middle eastern Chickpea Croutons.............................44
17. Felafel..46
18. Boiled Channa..48
HUMMUS..50
19. Chickpea Hummus with aquafaba..............................51
20. Veggie-Loaded Hummus..53
21. Beet Hummus...55
22. Courgette and Chickpea Hummus...............................57
23. Lemony Chickpea and Tahini Hummus......................59
24. Garlicky Chickpea Hummus..61
25. Spirulina Hummus...63
26. Hibiscus Hummus..65
27. Passion Fruit Hummus..67

28. Moringa and beetroot hummus..........69
29. Hummus with pumpking and pomegranate..........71
30. Roasted carrot hummus..........73
SANDWICH AND BURGERS..........75
31. Golden Chickpea Burgers..........76
32. Curried Chickpea Patties..........78
33. Moroccan Yam Veggie Burgers..........80
34. Quinoa and Sweet Potato Burger..........83
35. Tastes like Tuna Salad Sandwiches..........86
MAIN COURSE..........88
36. Mixed Grain Chili..........89
37. Cabbage Rolls Stuffed With Bulgur and Chickpeas.....91
38. Quinoa chickpea Buddha bowl..........94
39. Couscous-Chickpea Loaf with Sun-dried tomatoes.......96
40. Eggplant with quinoa..........99
41. Penne with Chickpeas and Spinach..........101
42. Chickpea Loaf..........103
43. Chickpea Spinach Lasagna..........106
44. Pastitsio..........109
45. Fajitas with Microgreens & Chickpeas..........112
46. Crunchy Chickpea Tacos..........114
47. Lamb dhansak..........116
48. Copycat Ikea Veggie Balls..........119
49. Garbanzo Parsnip Gnocchi with Pomegranate..........121
50. Vegan Chickpea 'Tuna'..........124
51. Lamb and purslane with chickpeas..........126
52. Basmati & Wild Rice with Chickpeas, Currants & Herbs..........129
53. Wild Rice, Cabbage and Chickpea Pilaf..........132
54. Moroccan Chickpea Tagine..........134
55. Nohutlu Pilav..........137
56. Vegan Chickpea Enchiladas..........139
57. Socca with Caramelized Onions and Rosemary..........141
58. Basmati & Wild Rice with Chickpeas, Currants & Herbs..........144

SOUPS AND CURRY 147
59. Mexican Margarita Chickpea Soup 148
60. Chickpea, Pumpkin, and Coconut Curry 151
61. Chickpea curry with sea moss 153
62. Chickpea Mushroom Soup 155
63. Curried Chickpea Meatballs 157
64. Tortellini Soup 159
65. Spinach and beet soup 161
66. Moroccan Chickpea Stew 163
67. Indian Chickpea Curry 165
68. Chickpea Sweet Potato Stew 167
69. Chickpea & Farro Stew 169
70. Curry Chana Stew From Trinidad 172
71. Cauliflower soup with pomegranate 174
72. Watercress & chickpea soup with rose water 177
SALADS 180
73. Canned Chickpea and Tofu Cheese Salad 181
74. Loaded Greens and Seeds Salad 184
75. Couscous & Chick-Pea Salad 186
76. Cauliflower & Chickpeas Salad 188
77. Smoky chickpea tuna salad 190
78. Spiced Chickpeas & Vegetable Salad 192
BUDDHA BOWLS 195
79. Chickpea Bowl 196
80. Scrambled Chickpea Breakfast Bowls 198
81. Za'atar Chickpea Bowls 200
82. Cauliflower Falafel Power Bowls 203
83. Herbed Chickpea and Bulgur Bowls 206
84. Butternut Squash and Kale Bowls 208
85. Masala Chickpea Bowls 210
86. Moroccan-Spiced Chickpea Bowls 213
87. Beet Falafel Bowls 216
88. Harissa Chicken Bowls 219
89. Greek Power Bowls 222
DESSERT 225

90. Chickpea choco slices..226
91. Chickpea Chocolate Chip Cookies..............................228
92. Chickpea Blondies..230
93. Chickpea Chocolate Mousse......................................232
94. Chickpea Peanut Butter Cups....................................234
95. Chickpea Brownies...236
96. Chickpea Coconut Macaroons...................................238
97. Chickpea Pumpkin Pie Bars......................................240
DRINKS..242
98. Blackberry Marshmallow Cream Soda......................243
99. Butterfly Pea Dalgona coffee.....................................245
100. Aquafaba Whipped Coffee.......................................247
CONCLUSION..249

INTRODUCTION

Welcome to the wonderful world of chickpeas—a versatile superfood that has been enjoyed for centuries across cultures and cuisines. In this cookbook, we embark on a culinary adventure that celebrates the incredible potential of chickpeas, offering you a treasure trove of recipes that will revolutionize the way you cook and eat.

Chickpeas, also known as garbanzo beans, are not only rich in nutrients but also incredibly adaptable. From hearty stews to vibrant salads, and from crispy snacks to indulgent desserts, chickpeas can elevate any dish with their unique flavor, texture, and nutritional benefits. Whether you're a dedicated vegan, a health-conscious foodie, or simply looking to add more plant-based protein to your diet, this cookbook is your guide to unlocking the full potential of chickpeas.

Within these pages, you'll find a diverse range of recipes that showcase the versatility of chickpeas. We'll take you on a journey through global cuisines, exploring dishes from the Mediterranean, the Middle East, India, and beyond. From creamy hummus and satisfying falafel to zesty chickpea curries and innovative chickpea-based baked goods, this cookbook has something for every taste and occasion.

So, join us as we dive into the world of chickpeas. We'll provide you with essential cooking tips, techniques, and creative ways to incorporate chickpeas into your favorite recipes. Get ready to savor the robust flavors, the satisfying textures, and the boundless culinary possibilities that chickpeas have to offer. Let's embark on this flavorful journey together!

BREAKFAST

1. Chickpea Crepe Tacos with Veal and Eggplant

INGREDIENTS:

- 2 ¼ cups of chickpea flour
- ¼ cup plain yogurt
- 2 ½ teaspoons salt (divided)
- 3 ½ tablespoons olive oil
- ¼ kg veal (ground)
- 1 ½ teaspoons cumin (ground)
- ¼ teaspoon red pepper flakes (crushed)
- 1 pound eggplant and cut them into cubes 1" in size
- 3 garlic cloves (sliced thinly)
- ¼ cup raisins (golden)
- ¼ cup red wine
- 15-ounce tomatoes (diced)
- ¼ cup pine nuts (toasted)

INSTRUCTIONS:

a) In a medium bowl, whisk the chickpea flour together with the yogurt, 1 ¼ teaspoon salt, and water (2 cups and 1 tablespoon) and set it aside.

b) Over a medium-high flame, in a large skillet, heat 1 tablespoon of oil. Add the veal, red pepper, cumin, and ¼ teaspoon salt to the skillet to cook the veal.

c) Make sure to break and stir the veal often so it does not clump together. As the veal begins to brown, (after about 4 minutes) remove the meat and spices from the skillet and place it in a medium bowl.

d) Heat 2 tablespoons oil on the skillet, before adding eggplant and the remaining salt. Cook the eggplant for 5 minutes or until it turns brown from all sides.

e) Now add garlic and stir occasionally until it turns a light brown color.

f) Add raisins and wine to cook the mixture. Remember to stir continuously, for a minute, so the mixture is heated uniformly.

g) Add the diced tomatoes (with juice), the lamb mixture, pine nuts, and $\frac{1}{4}$

h) cup water. Stir and reduce the heat to medium flame so the mixture

i) can simmer. Stir occasionally. In about 15 minutes, as most of the juices evaporate, close the flame.

j) Swirl the remaining oil in an 8" non-stick skillet, wipe it with a paper towel to leave just a sheen of oil on the skillet, and heat it to medium-high.

k) Whisking the flour mixture, pour about a third of a cup into the skillet.

l) Swirl to completely coat the pan with the batter, to make a crepe, cooking both sides until they are browned. Remove the crepe from the skillet and repeat the process with the remaining batter.

m) Spoon the lamb filling onto the pancakes.

2. Pane di Ceci

INGREDIENTS:
- 1½ cups chickpea flour
- 1¾ cups water
- 3 tablespoons extra-virgin olive oil
- 1 teaspoon salt
- Fresh rosemary or other herbs (optional)

INSTRUCTIONS:
a) In a mixing bowl, combine the chickpea flour and water. Whisk well until the mixture is smooth and free of lumps. Let it rest for at least 1 hour or up to overnight to allow the flour to hydrate.

b) Preheat the oven to 220°C (425°F) and place a large cast-iron skillet or baking dish in the oven to heat.

c) After the resting time, skim off any foam that may have formed on top of the chickpea batter.

d) Add the olive oil and salt to the batter and whisk until well combined.

e) Remove the heated skillet or baking dish from the oven and carefully pour the batter into it, spreading it evenly.

f) If desired, sprinkle fresh rosemary or other herbs over the top of the batter.

g) Place the skillet or baking dish back in the oven and bake for about 20-25 minutes, or until the edges are crispy and golden brown.

h) Remove the Pane di Ceci from the oven and let it cool for a few minutes before slicing it into wedges or squares.

i) Serve warm or at room temperature as a side dish, appetizer, or snack.

j) Serve with green vegetables, yogurt, and lemon wedges.

3.Mushrooms Chickpea Crêpes

INGREDIENTS:
CRÊPES:
- 140 g chickpea flour
- 30 g peanut flour
- 5 g nutritional yeast
- 5 g curry powder
- 350 ml water
- Salt, to taste

FILLING:
- 10 ml olive oil
- 4 Portobello mushroom caps, thinly sliced
- 1 onion, thinly sliced
- 30 g baby spinach
- Salt, and pepper, to taste
- Vegan mayo

INSTRUCTIONS:
MAKE THE CRÊPES
a) Combine chickpea flour, peanut flour, nutritional yeast, curry powder, water, and salt to taste in a food blender.
b) Heat a large non-stick skillet over medium-high heat. Spray the skillet with some cooking oil.
c) Pour ¼ cup of the batter into the skillet and with a swirl motion distribute the batter all over the skillet's bottom.
d) Cook the Crêpe for 1 minute per side. Slide the Crêpe onto a plate and keep warm.

MAKE THE FILLING
e) Heat olive oil in a skillet over medium-high heat.
f) Add mushrooms and onion and cook for 6-8 minutes.
g) Add spinach and toss until wilted, for 1 minute.
h) Season with salt and pepper and transfer into a large bowl.
i) Fold in prepared vegan mayo.

4. Chickpea Flour Crêpes

INGREDIENTS:
- ½ teaspoon ground coriander
- ½ teaspoon turmeric powder
- 2 green Thai, serrano, or cayenne chiles, chopped
- ¼ cup dried fenugreek leaves
- 2 cups gram flour
- 1 teaspoon red chile powder or cayenne
- Oil, for pan frying
- 1-piece ginger root, peeled and grated or minced
- ½ cup fresh cilantro, minced
- 1 teaspoon coarse sea salt
- 1½ cups water
- 1 onion, peeled and minced

INSTRUCTIONS:
a) In a large mixing bowl, combine the flour and water until smooth. Set aside.
b) Mix in the remaining ingredients, except the oil.
c) Preheat a griddle over medium heat.
d) Spread ½ teaspoon oil over the griddle.
e) Pour batter into the center of the pan.
f) Spread the batter in a circular, clockwise motion from the center to the outside of the pan with the back of the ladle to make a thin, round pancake.
g) Cook the poora for about 2 minutes on one side, then flip it to cook on the other side.
h) With the spatula, press down to ensure that the center is also cooked through.
i) Serve with Mint or Peach Chutney on the side.

5. Chickpea Milk

INGREDIENTS:
- 3 cups dried chickpeas
- 4 Medjool dates pitted
- 1 cup filtered water
- 1 teaspoon vanilla extract
- $\frac{1}{2}$ teaspoon cinnamon
- $\frac{1}{8}$ teaspoon ground nutmeg
- $\frac{1}{4}$ teaspoon salt
- $\frac{1}{2}$ gallon water

INSTRUCTIONS

a) Soak the chickpeas in water overnight. They will expand to about three times their original size. Drain any excess water from the chickpeas.

b) Add to blender or food processor, and blend until smooth. Add dates and blend for 2 minutes, gradually adding filtered water to help form a paste.

c) In a large pot, bring the remaining water to a boil. Add the chickpea paste, vanilla extract, salt, cinnamon, and nutmeg.

d) Reduce heat and simmer for 20-30 minutes, combining well so all ingredients are properly mixed.

e) Strain the mixture through a fine-mesh strainer or a clean mesh cloth. Discard the solids and store the liquid chickpea milk in an airtight container. Chill in the refrigerator for 2 hours before serving.

6. Wheat & Meat Porridge

INGREDIENTS:

- 1 pound of lamb's shoulder and back
- 2 ounces dried chickpeas
- 4 ounces dried wheat grains (red wheat is good)
- 2 medium onions
- 3 tablespoons vegetable oil
- 1/2 teaspoon turmeric
- Garnish: Icing sugar, cinnamon powder, and melted butter to taste

INSTRUCTIONS:

a) Wash and rinse the wheat and chickpeas separately and soak them in cold water overnight.
b) The next day, skin the peas and the wheat.
c) Wash and dry the meat and cut into chunks.
d) Peel and cut the onions into six chunks.
e) Heat the oil in a medium size pan and fry the onions until translucent.
f) Mix in the turmeric and add the meat chunks. Stir well to seal the meat on all sides.
g) Drain and add the chickpeas to the meat and mix well. Pour one pint of water or stock in the pot and bring to boil. Season to taste.
h) Reduce the heat and let simmer until the meat is nearly cooked. Sieve and add the wheat to the mix and let simmer until all the ingredients are thoroughly cooked. Add water as necessary and stir frequently during cooking.
i) Once cooked, pour the mixture into a pot and pound with the flat end of a steak tenderizer until the meat is shredded and a sticky porridge-like consistency is achieved. If the mixture is looser than the porridge, pour it back into the pan and return to low heat. Stir continuously until thicker and add icing sugar to taste.

j) Pour into individual bowls. Garnish with a sprinkling of cinnamon and icing sugar and a knob of butter before serving.

SNACKS

7. Roasted Chickpeas with aquafaba

INGREDIENTS:
- Two 15-oz cans of cooked chickpeas
- ½ lime, juiced
- 2 teaspoons chili flakes
- 1 tablespoon sweet paprika
- 2 teaspoons cumin
- 2 teaspoons garlic powder
- 2 teaspoons salt

AQUAFABA
- 2 tablespoons chickpea liquid

INSTRUCTIONS
FOR THE AQUAFABA:
a) Lightly whisk the liquid until foamy, then measure out the required amount of aquafaba.

FOR THE ROASTED CHICKPEAS:
b) Prepare a baking sheet with parchment paper and preheat the oven to 400° F.

c) Place the dry chickpeas in a single layer on the prepared baking sheet and bake for 25 minutes.

d) Whisk together the aquafaba, lime juice, chili flakes, paprika, cumin, garlic, and salt.

e) Drizzle the aquafaba-mixture over the half-roasted chickpeas, and toss well.

f) Return them to the baking sheet in a single layer and roast for 15 minutes more, or until crispy and golden.

g) Set aside for at least 10 minutes before serving to allow the chickpeas to cool.

8. Quinoa stuffed onions

INGREDIENTS:
- 12 mediums Onions; peeled
- ½ cup Quinoa; cooked
- 1 cup; water
- ¼ teaspoon Sea salt
- 2 Garlic cloves; minced (opt)
- ½ cup Mushrooms; sliced
- ½ cup Celery; sliced
- 2 tablespoons Corn or olive oil
- ½ cup Chickpeas; cooked
- 1 cup Walnuts; roasted
- 2 teaspoons Soy sauce
- 2 teaspoons Brown rice vinegar

INSTRUCTIONS:
a) Hollow out insides of onions with an apple corer, leaving bottoms intact and reserving insides. Steam hollowed-out onions until tender, reserving ¾ cup of cooking liquid.

b) Finely chop reserved onions. Sauté chopped onions, garlic, mushrooms and celery in oil for 15 minutes or until soft. Mix in quinoa and chickpeas and heat through (about 5 minutes).

c) Fill onions with quinoa mixture. Crush walnuts in a food processor blending in soy sauce and vinegar to form a creamy mixture. Blend in reserved cooking liquid. Place mixture in a saucepan and heat through, stirring constantly. Pour over stuffed onions, garnish and serve.

9. Pakora

INGREDIENTS:
- 1 cup Chickpea flour
- ½ cup Unbleached all-purpose flour
- ½ teaspoon Baking soda
- ¾ teaspoon Cream of tartar
- ¼ teaspoon Sea salt
- 1 teaspoon Cumin powder and Coriander powder
- 1 teaspoon Turmeric and Cayenne pepper
- 2 tablespoons Lemon juice
- 1 cup Sliced potatoes
- 1 cup Cauliflower florets
- 1 cup Chopped bell pepper

INSTRUCTIONS:
a) Blend flour, baking soda, cream of tartar, salt, and spices.

b) Gradually whisk in water and lemon juice to make a smooth batter with the consistency of heavy cream. Set aside.

c) Dip vegetables in the batter to coat. Immerse in hot oil, turning to cook evenly, until golden brown, about 5 minutes.

d) Remove with a slotted spoon and drain on absorbent paper.

10. Chickpea fritters with couscous

INGREDIENTS:
- 7 ounces Couscous, cooked
- ½ small Cucumber
- 2 Plum tomatoes; (peeled, seeded, diced)
- 1 Lime
- 6 Green onions; trimmed
- 1 can (14oz) chickpeas drained and rinsed
- ½ teaspoon Coriander or cilantro and mint
- 1 Red chili; seeded and finely chopped
- 1 Garlic clove
- Plain flour for dusting
- 5 ounces FF yogurt
- Salt and freshly ground pepper
- Paprika/Cumin to taste

INSTRUCTIONS:
a) Stir tomatoes, and parsley into couscous. Halve the lime and squeeze in the juice.
b) Finely chop spring onions into couscous.
c) Add cumin, coriander/cilantro, chili, and coriander/cilantro leaves.
d) Chop garlic clove and add. Place cucumber in a bowl and stir in yoghurt chop mint add with plenty of seasoning. Mix well
e) Shape the chickpea mixture into 6 patties and dust lightly with flour.
f) Add to the pan and cook for a few minutes.

11. Chickpea Blinis with Mustard Micros

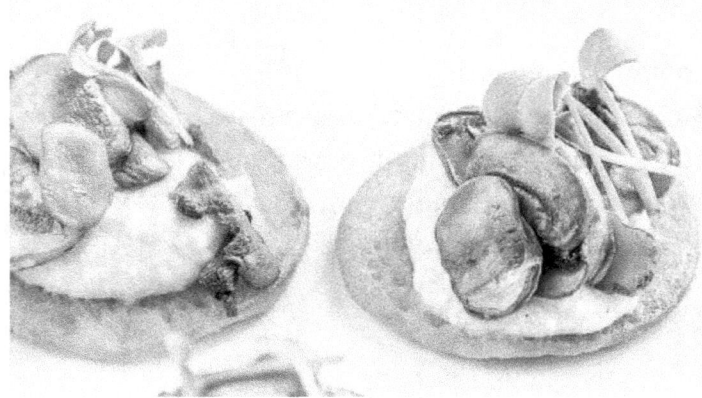

INGREDIENTS:
BLINIS
- 1 cup chickpea flour
- 1 egg
- ½ cup of water
- 1 tablespoon of olive oil
- 1 teaspoon of salt
- 2 green onions, chopped

AVOCADO CREAM CHEESE
- 2 tablespoons of fat-free cream cheese
- ½ avocado
- 1 green onion, chopped
- 1 teaspoon of salt
- Juice of ½ lime

TOPPINGS
- 1 Handful of Mustard Greens
- Avocado
- Swiss Cheese
- Pomegranate seeds

INSTRUCTIONS:
a) To make the blinis, whisk together 1 egg, ½ cup water, chopped green onions, and olive oil in a mixing bowl.

b) Combine the chickpea flour, salt, and pepper in a separate bowl. Add the wet mixture and beat until it is completely combined.

c) Pour 2 tablespoons of the mixture into the center of a non-stick skillet and heat over medium-high heat. Allow at least 5 minutes for the mixture to solidify into pancakes or blinis before turning it over.

d) Flip it over and cook for another 3 minutes until it has set and small bubbles develop on the top.

e) Combine the avocado cream cheese ingredients in a mixing bowl.

f) To serve, spread avocado cream cheese on 1 blini and top with mustard microgreens and pomegranate seeds.

12. Chickpea Salad Crostini

INGREDIENTS:
- 1 baguette, cut into 12 slices
- 2 tablespoons extra virgin olive oil
- 1 15-ounce can of chickpeas, drained and rinsed
- 1 15-ounce can of black beans, drained and rinsed
- 1 8-ounce can of corn, drained and rinsed
- 1 4-ounce can of black olives, drained and sliced
- 1 tablespoon fresh lime juice
- 2 teaspoons flaxseed meal
- 1 teaspoon ground cumin
- $\frac{1}{4}$ teaspoon chili powder
- $\frac{1}{4}$ teaspoon onion powder
- $\frac{1}{4}$ teaspoon salt
- Fresh thyme, for garnish

INSTRUCTIONS:
CROSTINI TOASTS
a) Lay out the bread slices on a baking sheet. Lightly brush each slice of bread with oil.

b) Put the baking sheet under the broiler. Don't do anything else. Just stand there and keep checking the bread and don't let it burn. It only takes a couple of minutes.

c) After the toasts are lightly browned, remove the sheet from the oven. You can make these ahead of time and keep them in the refrigerator for later use, too.

TO ASSEMBLE
d) In a large bowl, mix all the remaining ingredients, except the thyme.

e) Top each toast with the chickpea mixture just before serving. Garnish with fresh thyme.

13. Panisse bruschetta with Basil Microgreens

INGREDIENTS:
TOPPING
- 2 teaspoon olive oil
- 1½ cups cremini mushrooms, sliced
- ½ teaspoon salt
- A 15-ounce can of cannellini beans, rinsed
- ¾ cup basil microgreens

CHICKPEA CAKES
- 1 cup chickpea flour
- 2 ¼ cups water
- 1 Tablespoon olive oil
- few pinches of salt and pepper

INSTRUCTIONS:

a) In a skillet, heat the olive oil, then add the sliced mushrooms. Sprinkle with salt.

b) After the mushrooms have cooled, combine them with the cannellini beans and basil microgreens.

c) Combine all of the chickpea cake ingredients in a mixing bowl.

d) Preheat an empty non-stick skillet over moderate heat to cook your chickpea batter.

e) Add a few teaspoons of olive oil to the pan and wait for it to warm up for another minute or two. When the Panisse touches the pan, you want it to sizzle.

f) Pour the batter into the skillet. Stir the batter constantly with a whisk until it thickens, then transfer to a heat-resistant rubber spatula to stir consistently for a few minutes more.

g) Let it cool slightly before covering it with plastic wrap, pressing it against the top to form a seal, and placing it in the refrigerator to chill entirely for an hour or overnight.

h) After the block has cooled, cut it in half and slice each half into ½-inch thick slices.

PANISSE

i) Preheat an empty skillet over moderate heat for a few minutes, then add 1 or 2 teaspoons of olive oil and the Panisse slices carefully.

j) Sauté for 3-5 minutes on each side, or until golden, and finish with your topping.

14. Chickpea Salad Pinwheels

INGREDIENTS:
- 2 15-ounce cans of chickpeas drained and rinsed
- 1 large avocado or 2 small avocados
- 1 jalapeño chopped
- ½ red onion chopped
- ¼ cup mustard
- ¼ cup vegan mayo
- pepper to taste
- garlic salt to taste
- hot sauce to taste
- 2 large tortillas or wraps
- 2 handfuls of baby spinach

INSTRUCTIONS:
a) Add the chickpeas to a bowl and mash with a fork.
b) Add avocado and mash until the avocado is combined.
c) Add in the jalapeño, red onion, mustard, vegan mayo, pepper, garlic salt, and hot sauce.
d) Stir to combine. Taste and adjust seasonings as needed. Place in the fridge for at least 30 minutes.
e) To assemble, spread an even layer of filling to the outer edges of the tortilla.
f) The top half of the filling with spinach.
g) Starting at the end with spinach, tightly roll the tortillas up until you the other end.
h) Use a sharp knife, and cut the wrap into 8 pieces.
i) Serve right away or place in an air-tight container in the fridge until ready to serve.

15. Spiced chilli chickpeas

INGREDIENTS:
- 3 cups cooked chickpeas
- 1 tablespoon olive oil
- 2 teaspoon cumin seeds
- 2 teaspoon nigella seeds
- 2 teaspoon chilli flakes, to taste
- Sea salt flakes

INSTRUCTIONS:
a) In a small roasting tray, pour the drained and washed chickpeas in a single layer.
b) Drizzle in the oil and sprinkle the cumin, nigella, and chili flakes on top. Toss in a generous pinch of sea salt flakes to combine.
c) Place the pan in a hot wood oven and roast the chickpeas for about 30 minutes, shaking the tin to mix them up every now and then to ensure equal cooking.
d) They should be crisp and a rich golden brown color. Allow it cool slightly before transferring to a serving bowl.

16. Middle eastern Chickpea Croutons

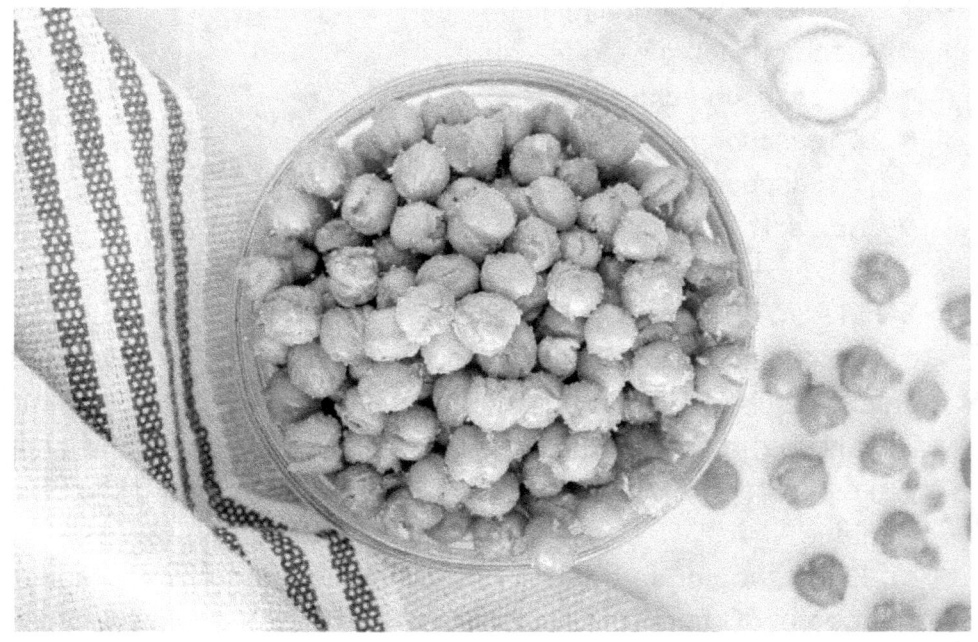

INGREDIENTS:
- 1 can (15 oz) chickpeas (garbanzo beans), drained and rinsed
- 2 tablespoons olive oil
- 1 teaspoon ground cumin
- 1 teaspoon ground coriander
- $\frac{1}{2}$ teaspoon ground paprika
- $\frac{1}{4}$ teaspoon ground turmeric
- $\frac{1}{4}$ teaspoon low-sodium salt
- $\frac{1}{4}$ teaspoon black pepper

INSTRUCTIONS:
a) Preheat the oven to 400°F (200°C) and line a baking sheet with parchment paper.
b) Drain and rinse the chickpeas. Pat them dry with a paper towel to remove excess moisture.
c) In a bowl, combine the olive oil, cumin, coriander, paprika, turmeric, salt, and black pepper. Stir well to create a spice mixture.
d) Add the chickpeas to the bowl with the spice mixture. Toss until the chickpeas are evenly coated with the spices.
e) Spread the seasoned chickpeas in a single layer on the prepared baking sheet.
f) Bake in the preheated oven for about 25-30 minutes, or until the chickpeas are crispy and golden brown. Stir the chickpeas halfway through the baking time to ensure even browning.
g) Remove the baking sheet from the oven and let the chickpea croutons cool slightly before serving.
h) Use the Middle Eastern Chickpea Croutons as a topping for salads, soups, or enjoy them as a crunchy snack.

17. Felafel

INGREDIENTS:
- 1 cup dried chickpeas, cooked
- 1 clove garlic, lightly crushed
- 1 medium onion, chopped
- 1 teaspoon ground coriander
- 1 teaspoon ground cumin
- 1-1/2 teaspoon cayenne pepper powder
- 1/2 cup chopped parsley leaves
- 1/2 teaspoon salt
- 1/2 teaspoon black pepper
- Juice of 1 whole lemon, squeezed
- Canola or corn oil for frying

INSTRUCTIONS:
a) Place chickpeas in the bowl of a food processor. Add remaining ingredients except oil. Pulse until finely chopped but not pureed, scraping sides of bowl down.
b) Add soaking water if necessary to allow mixture to form a ball—do not make a mushy paste.
c) Place about two inches of oil in a large, deep saucepan to a depth of at least two inches. Heat oil to about 350°F.
d) Form tablespoons of batter into the shape of balls or small patties. Fry in batches until browned, turning as necessary. Cooking time will be five minutes. Serve hot in pitta bread with chopped cucumbers and tomatoes, and humus dip.

18. Boiled Channa

INGREDIENTS:

- 2-3 tablespoon vegetable oil for frying
- 1 medium white onion, cut into thin rings
- 2 cans (15-16 ounces) chickpeas
- 1 red bird chili, finely chopped
- 1 teaspoon ground cumin
- 2 teaspoon ground coriander
- Salt to taste, if needed

INSTRUCTIONS:

a) Heat the oil in a wok or skillet.
b) Fry the onions until lightly browned.
c) Add the drained chickpeas and stir-fry briefly.
d) Add the chili and spices and continue to stir-fry for a minute or two.
e) Taste for salt and add some if needed. Canned chickpeas are usually salty enough.
f) Serve warm or at room temperature as a snack, with optional ready-made West Indian pepper sauce if you like your food very spicy. (Mexican habanero sauce is also good.)

HUMMUS

19. Chickpea Hummus with aquafaba

INGREDIENTS:
- 2 cups canned chickpeas
- 2 cloves garlic
- 4 tablespoons plant-based tahini
- 2 tablespoons lemon juice, freshly squeezed
- 2 teaspoons cumin powder
- 1 teaspoon salt
- ½ teaspoons chili powder

AQUAFABA
- ½ cup chickpea liquid

TOPPINGS
- Cilantro
- Coriander seeds
- Chili powder
- Whole chickpeas

INSTRUCTIONS:
TO MAKE THE AQUAFABA:
a) If the chickpea liquid contains a lot of small bits of beans, strain it through a fine mesh strainer to remove them.
b) Lightly whisk the liquid until foamy, then measure out the required amount of aquafaba.

TO MAKE THE HUMMUS:
c) Place the chickpeas, garlic, and aquafaba in a food processor jar and puree until smooth.
d) Add tahini, lemon juice, cumin, salt, and chili powder to taste.
e) Process on high speed until the hummus is smooth and creamy. If necessary, spritz with water.
f) Ladle the hummus into a serving bowl and top with fresh cilantro leaves and seeds.
g) Refrigerate in an airtight container for up to 5 days.

20. Veggie-Loaded Hummus

INGREDIENTS:
- 1 can chickpeas, drained and rinsed
- ½ cup cooked vegetables (e.g., carrots, peas, bell peppers)
- 2 tablespoons tahini
- 2 tablespoons lemon juice
- 2 tablespoons olive oil
- 1 clove garlic
- Salt and pepper to taste

INSTRUCTIONS:
a) In a food processor, combine the chickpeas, cooked vegetables, tahini, lemon juice, olive oil, garlic, salt, and pepper.
b) Blend until smooth and creamy, adding a little water if needed to reach the desired consistency.
c) Taste and adjust the seasoning if needed.
d) Pack the veggie-loaded hummus in a lunch container with cut-up veggies or pita bread for dipping.

21. Beet Hummus

INGREDIENTS:
- 1 can chickpeas, drained and rinsed
- 2 small beets, cooked and peeled
- 2 cloves garlic
- 2 tablespoons tahini
- 2 tablespoons lemon juice
- 2 tablespoons olive oil
- Salt and pepper to taste

INSTRUCTIONS:
a) In a food processor, combine the chickpeas, beets, garlic, tahini, lemon juice, olive oil, salt, and pepper.
b) Blend until smooth and creamy, adding a little water if needed to reach the desired consistency.
c) Taste and adjust the seasoning if needed.
d) Pack the beet hummus in a lunch container with cut-up veggies or pita bread for dipping.

22. Courgette and Chickpea Hummus

INGREDIENTS:
- 1 can of chickpeas, drained and rinsed
- 1 garlic clove, chopped
- 1 green courgette, chopped
- Handful chopped parsley
- Handful chopped basil
- Himalayan or Sea Salt
- Freshly ground black pepper
- 4 tablespoons olive oil
- A squeeze of fresh lemon juice

INSTRUCTIONS

a) Blend everything.

23. Lemony Chickpea and Tahini Hummus

INGREDIENTS:
- Lemon juice from ½ a lemon
- 1 can dried chickpeas, soaked
- 1 clove of garlic
- 1 tablespoon of tahini
- 1 tablespoon of olive oil

INSTRUCTIONS:

a) Blend everything until smooth.

24. Garlicky Chickpea Hummus

INGREDIENTS:
- 2 cloves of garlic
- 1 can of chick peas
- 1 tablespoon of Tahini
- Lemon juice from 1 Lemon
- 1 tablespoon olive oil

INSTRUCTIONS:
a) In a mixing bowl, blend all ingredients.

25. Spirulina Hummus

INGREDIENTS:
- 1 can chickpeas, drained, liquid reserved
- 1 tablespoon olive oil
- 2 teaspoons tahini
- 1 tablespoon freshly pressed lemon juice
- 1 clove garlic, crushed
- $\frac{1}{2}$ teaspoon salt

INSTRUCTIONS:
a) Place the chickpeas, olive oil, tahini, lemon juice, garlic, and salt in a food processor.

b) Turn on the food processor and slowly pour in some of the reserved chickpea liquid while the machine runs.

c) When the mixture is fully combined and smooth, transfer it into a serving dish.

26. Hibiscus Hummus

INGREDIENTS:
- 1 can (15 ounces) chickpeas, drained and rinsed
- 2 tablespoons tahini
- 2 tablespoons hibiscus syrup or hibiscus tea concentrate
- Juice of 1 lemon
- 1 clove garlic, minced
- 2 tablespoons olive oil
- Salt and pepper to taste
- Optional: paprika or drizzle of olive oil for garnish

INSTRUCTIONS:

a) In a food processor, combine the chickpeas, tahini, hibiscus syrup or tea concentrate, lemon juice, minced garlic, and olive oil.

b) Process until smooth and creamy, adding a little water if needed to achieve the desired consistency.

c) Season with salt and pepper to taste.

d) Transfer the hibiscus hummus to a serving bowl.

e) Optional: Garnish with a sprinkle of paprika or a drizzle of olive oil.

f) Serve the hibiscus hummus with pita bread, carrot sticks, or your favorite veggies for a tasty and nutritious snack.

27. Passion Fruit Hummus

INGREDIENTS:
- 1 can chickpeas, drained and rinsed
- ¼ cup tahini
- ¼ cup passion fruit pulp
- 2 cloves garlic, minced
- ¼ cup olive oil
- Salt and pepper to taste

INSTRUCTIONS:

a) In a food processor, combine the chickpeas, tahini, passion fruit pulp, garlic, olive oil, salt, and pepper.
b) Process until smooth and creamy.
c) Chill in the refrigerator for at least 30 minutes before serving.
d) Serve with pita chips or fresh vegetables.

28. Moringa and beetroot hummus

INGREDIENTS:
- 1/2 teaspoon Moringa powder
- 400g tin chickpeas, drained and rinsed
- 250g cooked beetroot
- 1 garlic clove
- 2 tablespoons tahini
- 2 teaspoon ground cumin
- 100ml extra virgin olive oil
- Juice of lemon
- Salt to taste

INSTRUCTIONS:
a) Add all the ingredients except the chickpeas into your blender/food processor. Mix until smooth.
b) Add the chickpeas and blend again until smooth and delicious!

29. Hummus with pumpking and pomegranate

INGREDIENTS:
- 1 cup Cooked chickpeas
- 1 cup Pumpkin, cooked and mashed, or canned pumpkin
- 2 tablespoons Tahini, orig called for 1/3 cup
- $\frac{1}{4}$ cup Fresh parsley, minced
- 3 Cloves garlic, minced
- 2 Pomegranates

INSTRUCTIONS:
a) Pita bread, split and warmed, or other crackers, bread, veggies
b) Puree the chickpeas, pumpkin, tahini, parsley, and garlic until smooth.
c) Transfer to a serving plate.
d) Bread open the pomegranates and separate the seeds from the inner membranse. Sprinkle he seeds over the hummus serv chilled or at room temperature with the pitas or other "dippers".

30. Roasted carrot hummus

INGREDIENTS:
- 1 can of chickpeas, rinsed and drained
- 3 carrots
- 1 clove garlic
- 1 teaspoon of paprika
- 1 loaded tablespoon of tahini
- The juice of 1 lemon
- 2 Tablespoons of additional virgin olive oil
- 6 Tablespoons of water
- 1/2 teaspoons cumin powder
- Salt to taste

INSTRUCTIONS:
a) Preheat the oven to 400 degrees Fahrenheit.
b) Wash and peel the carrots, then chop them into little pieces and place them on a baking dish with olive oil, a touch of salt, and half a teaspoon of paprika.
c) Bake for 35 minutes, or until carrots are tender.
d) Remove them from the oven and set them aside to cool.
e) Prepare the hummus while they cool: wash and drain the chickpeas thoroughly before putting them in a food mill with the rest of the active components. Process until you have a well-combined mixture.
f) After that, add the carrots and garlic and repeat the procedure!

SANDWICH AND BURGERS

31. Golden Chickpea Burgers

INGREDIENTS:
- 2 tablespoons olive oil
- 1 yellow onion, chopped
- 1/2 yellow bell pepper, chopped
- 1 1/2 cup cooked chickpeas
- 3/4 teaspoon salt
- 1/4 teaspoon freshly ground black pepper
- 1/4 cup wheat gluten flour
- Condiments of choice

INSTRUCTIONS:
a) In a skillet, heat 1 tablespoon of the oil and overheat. Add the onion and pepper and cook until softened, about 5 minutes. Set aside to cool slightly.
b) Transfer the cooled onion mixture to a food processor. Add the chickpeas, salt, and black pepper and pulse to mix. Add the flour and process to combine.
c) Shape the mixture into 4 burgers, about 4 inches in diameter. If the mixture is too loose, add a little extra flour.
d) In a skillet, heat the remaining 2 tablespoons of oil overheat.
e) Add the burgers and cook until firm and browned on both sides, turning once, about 5 minutes per side.
f) Serve the burgers with the condiments of your choice.

32. Curried Chickpea Patties

INGREDIENTS:
- 3 tablespoons olive oil
- 1 onion, chopped
- 11/2 teaspoons hot or mild curry powder
- 1/2 teaspoon salt
- 1/8 teaspoon ground cayenne
- 1 cup cooked chickpeas
- 1 tablespoon chopped fresh parsley
- 1/2 cup wheat gluten flour
- 1/3 cup dry unseasoned almond flour
- Lettuce leaves
- 1 ripe tomato, cut into 1/4-inch slices

INSTRUCTIONS:
a) In a skillet, heat 1 tablespoon of the oil and overheat. Add the onion, cover, and cook until softened, 5 minutes. Stir in 1 teaspoon of the curry powder, salt, and cayenne and remove from the heat. Set aside.
b) In a food processor, combine the chickpeas, parsley, wheat gluten flour, almond flour, and cooked onion. The process to combine, leaving some texture.
c) Form the chickpea mixture into 4 equal patties and set aside.
d) In a skillet, heat the remaining 2 tablespoons of oil overheat. Add the patties, cover, and cook until golden brown on both sides, turning once, about 5 minutes per side.
e) In a bowl, combine the remaining 1/2 teaspoon of curry powder with the mayonnaise, stirring to blend.
f) Serve burger with lettuce, and tomato slices.

33. Moroccan Yam Veggie Burgers

INGREDIENTS:
- 1.5 cups grated yam
- 2 garlic cloves, peeled
- ¾ cup fresh cilantro leaves
- 1 piece of fresh ginger, peeled
- 15-ounce can of chickpeas, drained and rinsed
- 2 tablespoons ground flax mixed with 3 tablespoons water
- ¾ cup rolled oats, ground into a flour
- ½ tablespoon sesame oil
- 1 tablespoon coconut aminos or low-sodium tamari
- ½-¾ teaspoon fine grain sea salt or pink Himalayan salt, to taste
- Freshly ground black pepper, to taste
- 1 ½ teaspoon chili powder
- 1 teaspoon cumin
- ½ teaspoon coriander
- ¼ teaspoon cinnamon
- ¼ teaspoon turmeric
- ½ cup cilantro-lime tahini sauce

INSTRUCTIONS:
a) Preheat the oven to 350F. Line a baking sheet with a piece of parchment paper.
b) Peel the yam. Using the regular-sized grate hole, grate the yam until you have 1 ½ lightly packed cups. Place into a bowl.
c) Remove the grater attachment from the food processor, and add the regular "s" blade. Mince the garlic, cilantro, and ginger until finely chopped.
d) Add drained chickpeas and process again until finely chopped, but leave some texture. Scoop this mixture into a bowl.
e) In a bowl, stir together the flax and water mixture.
f) Grind the oats into flour using a blender or a food processor. Or you can use ¾ cup + 1 tablespoon of pre-

ground oat flour. Stir this into the mixture along with the flax mixture.
g) Now stir in the oil, aminos/tamari, salt/pepper, and spices until thoroughly combined. Adjust to taste if desired.
h) Shape 6-8 patties, packing the mixture firmly together. Place on baking sheet.
i) Bake for 15 minutes, then carefully flip, and bake for another 18-23 minutes until golden and firm. Cool on pan.

34. Quinoa and Sweet Potato Burger

INGREDIENTS:
- 3 medium sweet potatoes, baked
- 2 eggs
- 1 cup chickpea flour
- 1 teaspoon chili powder
- 1 tablespoon wholegrain Dijon mustard
- 1 tablespoon Walnut Butter or other Nut Butter
- juice of ½ lemon
- 1 pinch of sea salt
- 200 g quinoa
- peanut oil, for frying
- Horseradish sour cream
- 3 tablespoons finely grated horseradish
- 1¼ cups sour cream
- sea salt

TO SERVE
- 6 burger buns, halved
- butter for the buns
- finely sliced red Asian shallots
- finely chopped chives

INSTRUCTIONS:
a) Split the potatoes lengthwise and use a spoon to scrape out the insides.
b) Blend the eggs in a food processor and blend in the sweet potatoes, chickpea flour, chili powder, mustard, Nut Butter, lemon juice, and salt. Add the quinoa.
c) Using a handful of the mixture at a time, form round patties.
d) In a mixing bowl, combine the salt, horseradish, and sour cream.
e) Over medium heat, grill the patties for a few minutes on both sides.
f) Butter the cut surfaces of the buns and rapidly grill them.

g) Place a burger on the bottom of each bun, and cover it with horseradish sour cream, shallots, and chives.

35. Tastes like Tuna Salad Sandwiches

INGREDIENTS:
- 1 1/2 cups cooked or 1 (15.5-ounce) can chickpeas, drained and rinsed
- 2 celery ribs, minced
- 1/4 cup minced onion
- 1 teaspoon capers, drained and chopped
- 1 cup vegan mayonnaise
- 2 teaspoons fresh lemon juice
- 1 teaspoon Dijon mustard
- 1 teaspoon kelp powder
- 4 lettuce leaves
- 4 slices ripe tomato
- Salt and pepper
- Bread

INSTRUCTIONS:

a) In a medium bowl, coarsely mash the chickpeas. Add the celery, onion, capers, 1/2 cup of the mayonnaise, lemon juice, mustard, and kelp powder.

b) Season with salt and pepper to taste. Mix until well combined.

c) Cover and refrigerate at least 30 minutes to allow flavors to blend.

d) When ready to serve, spread the remaining 1/4 cup mayonnaise onto 1 side of each of the bread slices. Layer lettuce and tomato on 4 of the bread slices and evenly divide the chickpea mixture among them.

e) Top each sandwich with the remaining slice of bread, mayonnaise side down, cut in half, and serve.

MAIN COURSE

36. Mixed Grain Chili

INGREDIENTS:
- 2 tablespoons olive oil
- 2 shallots, chopped
- 1 large yellow onion, diced
- 1 tablespoon fresh ginger, finely grated
- 8 garlic cloves, crushed
- 1 teaspoon ground cumin
- 3 tablespoons red pepper powder
- Salt
- Black pepper
- 28-ounce can of crushed tomatoes
- 1 canned chipotle pepper, chopped
- 1 Serrano pepper, seeded and chopped
- 3 chopped spring onions
- ⅔ cup bulgur
- ⅔ cup pearl barley
- 2¼ cups mixed lentils, rinsed
- 1½ cups canned chickpeas

INSTRUCTIONS:
a) Heat the oil In a skillet over high heat and cook the shallot and onion for 4-5 minutes.
b) Sauté for 1 minute with ginger, garlic, cumin, and chili powder.
c) Combine with the tomatoes, peppers, and broth.
d) Bring the ingredients to a boil, excluding the spring onion.
e) Reduce to low heat and cook for 35 to 45 minutes, or until desired thickness is reached.
f) Serve hot and sprinkle with spring onions.

37. Cabbage Rolls Stuffed With Bulgur and Chickpeas

INGREDIENTS:
- 1 large head green cabbage, cored
- 1 tablespoon olive oil
- 1 medium yellow onion, minced
- 1 cup medium-grind bulgur
- 2 cups water
- Salt
- 1 1/2 cups cooked or 1 (15.5-ounce) can chickpeas, drained, rinsed, and mashed
- 2 tablespoons minced fresh dillweed or 1 tablespoon dried
- Freshly ground black pepper
- 2 cups tomato juice

INSTRUCTIONS:
a) Carefully remove 12 large leaves from the cabbage, reserving the remaining cabbage for another use. Steam the cabbage leaves until softened, 8 to 10 minutes. Set aside to cool.
b) In a large saucepan, heat the oil over medium heat. Add the onion and cook, covered, until softened, about 5 minutes. Stir in the bulgur, water, and 1/2 teaspoon of salt. Bring to a boil. Cover,
c) reduce heat to low, and simmer until the bulgur has absorbed the water, about 15 minutes.
d) Transfer to a large bowl. Add the beans to the bulgur mixture along with the dillweed and salt and pepper to taste. Mix well.
e) Place the cabbage leaves, one a time, on a flat work surface, rib side down. Place about 1/3 cup of the stuffing mixture at the stem end of each leaf.
f) Beginning at the stem end, roll up the leaf around the stuffing, tucking in the sides of the leaf as you roll it up. Repeat the process with the remaining leaves and stuffing.

g) Pour 1 cup of the tomato juice into a large deep skillet with a lid. Arrange the stuffed cabbage rolls in the pot, seam side down. Pour the remaining 1 cup tomato juice over the cabbage rolls. Cover and cook over low heat until tender, 20 to 30 minutes. Serve immediately.

38. Quinoa chickpea Buddha bowl

INGREDIENTS:
SALAD:
- 1 cup dry chickpeas, cooked
- 1 cup white quinoa, cooked
- 1 big package curly kale

TAHINI SAUCE:
- 1/2 cup tahini
- 1/4 teaspoon sea salt
- 1/4 teaspoon garlic powder
- 1/4 cup water
- Fresh lemon juice

INSTRUCTIONS:
TO MAKE DRESSING:
a) Combine tahini, sea salt, lemon juice and garlic powder in a little mixing bowl and whisk to integrate. Then add water a little at a time till it forms a pourable sauce.
b) Add 1/2-inch water to a medium pan and add the kale. Bring to a simmer over medium heat.
c) Instantly remove the kale from the heat and transfer to a small dish.

TO ASSEMBLE THE SALAD:
d) Combine the cooked chickpea, quinoa and kale in a bowl. Toss in the dressing.

39.Couscous-Chickpea Loaf with Sun-dried tomatoes

INGREDIENTS:
- 2 cups vegetable broth
- 1 cup couscous
- Salt
- 1 tablespoon olive oil
- 3 garlic cloves, minced
- 1½ cups cooked chickpeas
- 14.5-ounce can diced tomatoes, drained
- ¼ cup minced oil-packed Sun-dried tomatoes
- 1 tablespoon chopped capers
- 1 teaspoon dried basil
- ½ teaspoon dried oregano
- Freshly ground black pepper
- 10 ounces firm tofu, drained and patted dry

INSTRUCTIONS:
a) In a large saucepan, bring the broth to a boil over high heat. Add the couscous and salt to taste. Turn off the heat, cover, and let sit for 10 minutes.

b) Preheat the oven to 350°F. Lightly oil a 9-inch loaf pan and set it aside. In a large skillet, heat the oil over medium heat.

c) Add the garlic and cook until softened, about 30 seconds. Add the chickpeas, tomatoes, Sun-dried tomatoes, capers, basil, oregano, and salt and pepper to taste.

d) Stir to mix well, then reduce heat to low and simmer until the liquid evaporates, about 5 minutes. Set aside.

e) In a blender or food processor, combine the tofu, 1 cup of the chickpea mixture, and salt and pepper to taste. Process until smooth and stir back into the chickpea mixture.

f) In a large bowl, combine the cooked couscous with the chickpea and tofu mixture and transfer to the prepared loaf pan.

g) Cover and bake for 25 minutes. Uncover and continue baking until the top is lightly browned, about 10 minutes longer.

h) Allow to sit at room temperature for 15 minutes and then slice and serve.

40. Eggplant with quinoa

INGREDIENTS:
- 2 Eggplants, boiled
- 1 cup Quinoa, cooked
- 1 small Onion
- 2 Garlic cloves; minced
- 1 Poblano pepper
- 1 Banana or Hungarian pepper
- ½ cup Tomato puree or tomato sauce
- Fresh pepper and salt to taste
- ¼ cup Ground walnuts
- 1 cup Cooked chickpeas
- Pinch Wheat flour and Gluten flour

INSTRUCTIONS:
a) Chop the eggplant insides and set aside to sauté.
b) In a large frying pan, add the water and heat over medium heat. Then add the onion, garlic, peppers, and the eggplant insides, and sauté, adding a little more water as needed.
c) Then add the tomato puree, salt, pepper, walnuts, and chickpeas.
d) Cover and simmer about 5 minutes, stirring occasionally. Add the cooked quinoa, wheat flour, and gluten flour to the vegetable sauté and stir well. Fill the eggplant shells with the quinoa mixture. Bake.

41. Penne with Chickpeas and Spinach

INGREDIENTS:
- 1 medium yellow onion, peeled and diced
- 4 cloves garlic, peeled and minced
- ½ cup dry white wine
- 6 Sun-dried tomatoes, soaked in hot water, drained, and chopped
- ½ pound baby spinach (about 3 cups packed)
- ¼ cup chopped dill
- 2 cups cooked chickpeas, or one 15-ounce can, drained and rinsed
- Salt and freshly ground black pepper
- 12 ounces whole-grain penne, cooked, drained, and kept warm
- Salt and freshly ground black pepper to taste

INSTRUCTIONS:
a) Place the onion in a large skillet or saucepan and sauté over medium heat for 10 minutes.

b) Add water 1 to 2 tablespoons at a time to keep from sticking to the pan. Add the garlic and cook for 3 minutes.

c) Add the white wine and Sun-dried tomatoes and cook until almost all the liquid has evaporated.

d) Add the spinach, dill, and chickpeas and cook until the spinach is wilted. Remove from the heat.

e) Add the cooked pasta, mix well, and season with salt and pepper.

42. Chickpea Loaf

INGREDIENTS:
- 1 large can of chickpeas
- 3 Tablespoons ground flaxseeds
- ½ cup cold water
- 1 Tablespoon oil
- 1 onion, diced
- Vegetable oil spray, if needed
- One 25-ounce can of chickpeas (garbanzos), drained and rinsed
- ¼ cup Chipotle Barbecue Sauce or Smooth Adobo Sauce
- 2 Tablespoons potato starch
- 1 cup crushed crackers, such as saltines
- ¼ cup chopped black olives
- ½ cup lightly toasted walnuts or pecans

INSTRUCTIONS:
a) Mix the flaxseeds and cold water in a blender or with a hand blender. Blend on high until the texture is very thick.

b) Heat a heavy skillet over medium heat. Add oil and onions and stir. Place a lid directly over the onions and sweat until the onions are transparent. Remove lid and continue to cook until onions brown.

c) Meanwhile, preheat the oven to 350 degrees. Oil a loaf pan or line it with parchment paper. Combine the chickpeas and sauce in a large bowl. Thoroughly mash chickpeas with a potato masher. Sprinkle potato starch and crackers over chickpeas. Stir in, and then add olives and nuts. When everything is blended, stir in the flaxseed-water mixture.

d) Press the mixture into the loaf pan. Bake for 1 hour or until browned on top. Remove the loaf from the oven and then from the pan. If the loaf needs further cooking, you can set it on a pizza screen and put it back in the oven for a few minutes.

e) When done, let it sit for 15-20 minutes before slicing. Top with your favorite gravy, tomato sauce, or adobo sauce.

43. Chickpea Spinach Lasagna

INGREDIENTS:
- 9 lasagna noodles
- 1 tablespoon olive oil
- 1 onion, diced
- 2 cloves garlic, minced
- 2 cans (15 ounces each) of chickpeas, drained and rinsed
- 1 can (14 ounces) diced tomatoes
- 2 cups tomato sauce
- 2 cups fresh spinach
- 1 teaspoon dried basil
- 1 teaspoon dried oregano
- Salt and pepper to taste
- 2 cups shredded mozzarella cheese (vegan, if desired)
- Fresh parsley leaves for garnish

INSTRUCTIONS:
a) Preheat your oven to 375°F (190°C).
b) Cook the lasagna noodles according to the package instructions. Drain and set aside.
c) In a large skillet, heat the olive oil over medium heat.
d) Add the diced onion and minced garlic to the skillet and sauté until softened.
e) Add the chickpeas, diced tomatoes, tomato sauce, fresh spinach, dried basil, dried oregano, salt, and pepper to the skillet. Stir well to combine.
f) Simmer the mixture for about 10 minutes, allowing the flavors to meld together and the spinach to wilt.
g) In a greased 9x13-inch baking dish, layer the lasagna noodles and chickpea-spinach mixture. Repeat the layers until all the ingredients are used, ending with a layer of cheese on top.
h) Cover the baking dish with foil and bake in the preheated oven for 25 minutes.

i) Remove the foil and bake for an additional 10 minutes, or until the cheese is melted and bubbly.
j) Let the lasagna cool for a few minutes before serving.
k) Garnish with fresh parsley leaves.

44. Pastitsio

INGREDIENTS:
- 3 cups cooked chickpeas, drained and rinsed
- 12 ounces elbow macaroni
- 1 tablespoon olive oil
- 1 medium yellow onion, chopped
- 2 garlic cloves, chopped
- 1 (10-ounce) package of frozen chopped spinach, thawed
- 1/2 teaspoon dried oregano
- 1/2 teaspoon ground cinnamon
- 1/2 teaspoon dried mint
- 1/4 cup dry white wine
- 2 cups marinara sauce
- 2 tablespoons chopped fresh flat-leaf parsley
- Salt and freshly ground black pepper
- 2 cups Vegan White Sauce
- 1/2 cup chopped pine nuts

INSTRUCTIONS

a) In a food processor, pulse the chickpeas until coarsely chopped and set aside.

b) In a pot of boiling salted water, cook the macaroni over medium-high heat, stirring occasionally, until al dente, about 8 minutes. Drain well and set aside. Preheat the oven to 375°F. Lightly oil a 9 x 13-inch baking dish and set aside.

c) In a large skillet, heat the oil over medium heat. Add the onion and garlic, cover, and cook until softened about 5 minutes. Stir in the spinach, chopped chickpeas, oregano, cinnamon, mint, and wine and simmer, uncovered, for 3 minutes. Stir in the tomato sauce, parsley, and salt and pepper to taste. Cook over low heat for 10 minutes to blend flavors.

d) Spread half of the cooked pasta in the prepared baking dish and spread the tomato-chickpea sauce on top. Spread the remaining pasta on top of the tomato-chickpea sauce and top the pasta with the white sauce. Sprinkle with pine nuts.

e) Cover with foil and bake for 30 minutes. Uncover and bake for 10 minutes longer. Let stand at room temperature for 10 minutes before serving.

45. Fajitas with Microgreens & Chickpeas

INGREDIENTS:
- 3 bell peppers, sliced into strips
- ¼ teaspoon cumin
- 1 teaspoon fine sea salt
- 3 tablespoons olive oil
- 1 tablespoon chili powder
- 2 cups cooked chickpeas
- ½ teaspoon garlic powder
- 1 yellow onion, sliced into strips
- 8 corn tortillas

TO GARNISH
- A handful of fresh cilantro microgreens
- 1 tablespoon hot sauce

INSTRUCTIONS:
a) Preheat the oven to 450 degrees.
b) Arrange the pepper and onion strips onto a lined baking sheet along with the chickpeas.
c) Drizzle with olive oil and then sprinkle with chili powder, garlic powder, cumin, and salt.
d) Roast for 20 minutes, stirring regularly.
e) Serve with corn tortillas, fresh cilantro microgreens, and hot sauce.

46. Crunchy Chickpea Tacos

INGREDIENTS:
- 6 corn or flour tortillas
- One 15-ounce can of chickpeas, rinsed and drained
- ½ teaspoon ancho chili powder
- 3 cups shredded green cabbage
- 1 cup shredded carrot
- ½ cup thinly sliced red onion
- ½ cup seeded and small-diced poblano pepper
- ½ cup sliced green onion
- ¼ cup chopped fresh cilantro
- ¼ cup Tofu Cashew Mayonnaise 1 serving
- 2 tablespoons lime juice ¼ teaspoon sea salt
- 1 avocado, pitted and sliced
- 1 tablespoon Sriracha

INSTRUCTIONS:
a) Preheat the oven to 375°F.
b) Shape the tortillas by placing them in a nonstick oven-safe bowl and baking them in the oven until crispy, 5-10 minutes.
c) In a large mixing bowl, smash the chickpeas with a fork and sprinkle with the chili powder.
d) Add the cabbage, carrot, red onion, poblano pepper, green onion, cilantro, mayonnaise, and lime juice.
e) Mix thoroughly, adding salt last.
f) Divide the salad mixture among the taco bowls and top with the sliced avocado. Add Sriracha if you like your tacos spicy.

47. Lamb dhansak

INGREDIENTS:
- ¾ cup yellow lentils
- 2 teaspoons dried yellow mung beans
- 2 tablespoons dried chickpeas
- 3 tablespoons red lentils
- 1 unpeeled eggplant
- 5½ oz unpeeled pumpkin
- 2 tablespoons ghee or oil
- 1 onion, finely chopped
- 3 garlic cloves, crushed
- 1 tablespoon grated ginger
- 2 lb boneless leg or shoulder of lamb, cubed
- 1 cinnamon stick
- 5 cardamom pods, bruised
- 3 cloves
- 1 tablespoon ground coriander
- 1 teaspoon ground turmeric
- 1 teaspoon chili powder, or to taste
- 5½ oz amaranth or English spinach leaves, cut into 5 cm lengths
- 2 tomatoes, halved
- 2 long green chilies, seeded, split lengthways
- 3 tablespoons lime juice

INSTRUCTIONS:
a) Soak the yellow lentils, yellow mung beans, and chickpeas in water for about 2 hours, then drain well.

b) Put all four types of pulse in a saucepan, add water, cover and bring to a boil.

c) Uncover and simmer for 15 minutes, skimming off any scum that forms on the surface, and stirring occasionally to make sure all the pulses are cooking at the same rate and are soft. Drain the pulses and lightly mash them to a similar texture.

d) Cook the eggplant and pumpkin in boiling water for 10-15 minutes, or until soft. Scoop out the pumpkin flesh and cut it into pieces. Peel the eggplant carefully and cut the flesh into small pieces.

e) Heat the ghee or oil in a casserole dish or karahi and fry the onion, garlic, and ginger for 5 minutes, or until lightly brown and softened. Add the lamb and brown for 10 minutes, or until aromatic.

f) Add the cinnamon, cardamom pods, cloves, coriander, turmeric, and chili powder, and fry for 5 minutes to allow the flavors to develop. Add water, cover, and simmer for 40 minutes, or until the lamb is tender.

g) Add the mashed lentils and all the cooked and raw vegetables to the pan.

h) Add the lime juice and simmer for 15 minutes.

i) Stir well, then check the seasoning. The dhansak should be flavorsome, aromatic, tart, and spicy.

48. Copycat Ikea Veggie Balls

INGREDIENTS:
- 1 can Chickpeas, canned
- 1 cup Frozen spinach
- 3 Carrots
- ½ Bell Pepper
- ½ cup Canned Sweet corn
- 1 cup Green peas
- 1 Onion
- 3 cloves Garlic
- 1 cup Oat flour
- 1 tablespoon Olive oil
- Seasoning

INSTRUCTIONS:
a) Add all vegetables to a food processor and pulse until they are finely chopped.
b) Now add frozen, but thawed or fresh spinach, the dried sage, and the dried parsley.
c) Add the canned chickpeas & Pulse until they are combined.
d) Mix and cook for 1-2 minutes.
e) To make veggie balls, scoop a ball, and form it with your hands.
f) Place the balls on parchment paper or a baking sheet.
g) Bake them for 20 minutes until they have a crispy crust.

49. Garbanzo Parsnip Gnocchi with Pomegranate

INGREDIENTS:
- 2 cups cooked garbanzo beans (chickpeas), drained and rinsed
- 1 cup cooked parsnips, mashed
- 1 ½ cups all-purpose flour
- ¼ cup nutritional yeast (optional, for added flavor)
- 1 teaspoon salt
- ½ teaspoon garlic powder
- ¼ teaspoon black pepper
- Olive oil (for cooking)
- Your choice of sauce (e.g., marinara, pesto) for serving
- Pomegranate seeds (for serving)

INSTRUCTIONS:
a) In a large mixing bowl, combine the cooked garbanzo beans and mashed parsnips. Mash them together using a potato masher or fork until well combined.

b) Add the flour, nutritional yeast (if using), salt, garlic powder, and black pepper to the bowl. Stir well to combine and form a dough.

c) Dust a clean surface with flour and transfer the gnocchi dough onto it. Knead the dough gently for a few minutes until it becomes smooth and pliable. Be careful not to over-knead.

d) Divide the dough into smaller portions. Take one portion and roll it into a long rope about ½ inch thick. Repeat with the remaining dough.

e) Use a knife or bench scraper to cut the ropes into small pieces, about 1 inch in length. You can leave them as is or use the back of a fork to create ridges on each piece.

f) Bring a large pot of salted water to a boil. Add the gnocchi in batches, being careful not to overcrowd the pot. Cook the gnocchi for about 2-3 minutes or until they float to the surface. Once they float, cook for an additional 1 minute and then remove them using a slotted spoon or spider strainer. Repeat until all the gnocchi are cooked.

g) Heat some olive oil in a skillet over medium heat. Add the cooked gnocchi in a single layer and cook for a few minutes until they become lightly browned and crispy. Flip them over and cook for another minute or two. Repeat with the remaining gnocchi.

h) Serve the Garbanzo Parsnip Gnocchi hot with your choice of sauce, such as marinara or pesto.

i) You can also add some grated Parmesan cheese, pomegranate seeds, and fresh herbs for garnish if desired.

50. Vegan Chickpea 'Tuna'

INGREDIENTS:

- 15 ounce Can Chickpeas Drained, or 1 and ½ cups cooked chickpeas
- ¼ cup Vegan Mayonnaise
- 1 Nori Sheet Finely Chopped
- ¼ cup Red Onion Finely Chopped
- 1 tablespoon Lemon Juice
- 10 Capers Finely Chopped
- ½ teaspoons Garlic Powder
- 1 tablespoon Nutritional Yeast
- 1 tablespoon Tamari or Soy Sauce
- ½ tablespoons Dijon Mustard
- ½ teaspoons White Vinegar
- Sprinkle Sea Salt
- Sprinkle Ground Black Pepper

INSTRUCTIONS

- ☑ Add the chickpeas to a mixing bowl and mash them with a fork.
- ☑ Add in vegan mayonnaise, finely chopped nori, finely chopped red onion, lemon juice, finely chopped capers, garlic powder, nutritional yeast, tamari, Dijon mustard, white vinegar, and salt and pepper.
- ☑ Taste test and add more salt and pepper if needed.
- ☑ Mix in and you're ready to serve!

51. Lamb and purslane with chickpeas

INGREDIENTS:
- 3 tablespoons olive oil
- 1 Onion, diced
- 1 tablespoon Ground coriander
- $\frac{1}{2}$ tablespoon Ground cumin
- 1 kilogram of Lean lamb, diced
- $1\frac{1}{2}$ tablespoon tomato paste
- 30 grams Red pepper paste
- $\frac{1}{2}$ cup Green lentils, soaked overnight
- $\frac{3}{4}$ cup Chickpeas, soaked overnight
- $\frac{1}{2}$ cup Black-eyed peas, soaked overnight
- $\frac{1}{2}$ cup Coarse bulgar
- 4 Cloves garlic, minced
- 4 cups vegetable stock
- 1 kilograms Purslane, watercress, or silverbeet, washed and coarsely chopped
- Sea salt to taste
- 2 Lemons, juice only
- 4 tablespoons Olive oil
- 1 teaspoon Chilli flakes
- 2 teaspoons Dried mint

INSTRUCTIONS:
a) Heat the olive oil until smoking then adds the onions and sauté, until golden.
b) Add the coriander and cumin and mix briefly with the onions until fragrant then add the lamb and cook over high heat until the meat is cooked on the outside, about 5 minutes.
c) Add the lentils, chickpeas, and black-eyed peas and simmer the casserole for 25 minutes.
d) Add the garlic and bulgar and mix well, adding 2 cups water then continue simmering for about 20 minutes.

e) Season to taste and add the chopped greens and mix well to allow the greens to wilt, cook for a further two minutes.
f) To make the flavored oil, heat the oil with the chili flakes and mint until the oil begins to sizzle.
g) To serve, divide the casserole amongst dishes and drizzle about a tablespoon of the hot oil over the top.

52. Basmati & Wild Rice with Chickpeas, Currants & Herbs

INGREDIENTS:
- ⅓ cup / 50 g wild rice
- 2½ tbsp olive oil
- rounded 1 cup / 220 g basmati rice
- 1½ cups / 330 ml boiling water
- 2 tsp cumin seeds
- 1½ tsp curry powder
- 1½ cups / 240 g cooked and drained chickpeas (canned are fine)
- ¾ cup / 180 ml sunflower oil
- 1 medium onion, thinly sliced
- 1½ tsp all-purpose flour
- ⅔ cup / 100 g currants
- 2 tbsp chopped flat-leaf parsley
- 1 tbsp chopped cilantro
- 1 tbsp chopped dill
- salt and freshly ground black pepper

INSTRUCTIONS:
a) Start by putting the wild rice in a small saucepan, cover with plenty of water, bring to a boil, and leave to simmer for about 40 minutes, until the rice is cooked but still quite firm. Drain and set aside.
b) To cook the basmati rice, pour 1 tablespoon of the olive oil into a medium saucepan with a tightly fitting lid and place over high heat.
c) Add the rice and ¼ teaspoon salt and stir as you warm up the rice.
d) Carefully add the boiling water, decrease the heat to very low, cover the pan with the lid, and leave to cook for 15 minutes.
e) Remove the pan from the heat, cover with a clean tea towel and then the lid, and leave off the heat for 10 minutes.

f) While the rice is cooking, prepare the chickpeas. Heat the remaining $1\frac{1}{2}$ tbsp olive oil in a small saucepan over high heat. Add the cumin seeds and curry powder, wait for a couple seconds, and then add the chickpeas and $\frac{1}{4}$ teaspoon salt; make sure you do this quickly or the spices may burn in the oil. Stir over the heat for a minute or two, just to heat the chickpeas, then transfer to a large mixing bowl.
g) Wipe the saucepan clean, pour in the sunflower oil, and place over high heat. Make sure the oil is hot by throwing in a small piece of onion; it should sizzle vigorously. Use your hands to mix the onion with the flour to coat it slightly. Take some of the onion and carefully (it may spit!) place it in the oil. Fry for 2 to 3 minutes, until golden brown, then transfer to paper towels to drain and sprinkle with salt. Repeat in batches until all the onion is fried.
h) Finally, add both types of rice to the chickpeas and then add the currants, herbs, and fried onion. Stir, taste, and add salt and pepper as you like. Serve warm or at room temperature.

53. Wild Rice, Cabbage and Chickpea Pilaf

INGREDIENTS:
- ½ cup wild rice
- 1 medium onion, peeled and diced small
- 1 medium carrot, peeled and grated
- 1 small red bell pepper, seeded and diced small
- 3 cloves garlic, peeled and minced
- 1 tablespoon grated ginger
- 1½ cups chopped green cabbage
- 1 cup cooked chickpeas
- 1 bunch green onions (white and green parts), thinly sliced
- 3 tablespoons chopped cilantro
- Salt and freshly ground black pepper to taste

INSTRUCTIONS
a) Bring 2 cups of water to a boil in a large saucepan. Add the rice and bring the water back to a boil over high heat.
b) Reduce the heat to medium and cook the rice, covered, for 55 to 60 minutes. Drain off any excess water and set aside.
c) Heat a large skillet over a medium heat. Add the onion, carrot, and red pepper, and sauté the vegetables for 10 minutes. Add water 1 to 2 tablespoons at a time to keep the vegetables from sticking to the pan. Add the garlic and ginger and cook for another minute.
d) Add the cabbage and cook for 10 to 12 minutes, or until the cabbage is tender. Add the chickpeas, green onion, and cilantro.
e) Season with salt and pepper and cook for another minute to heat the chickpeas.
f) Remove from the heat, add the cooked wild rice, and mix well.

54. Moroccan Chickpea Tagine

INGREDIENTS:
- 2 tablespoons olive oil
- 1 onion, diced
- 3 cloves garlic, minced
- 1 teaspoon ground cumin
- 1 teaspoon ground coriander
- ½ teaspoon ground cinnamon
- ½ teaspoon ground ginger
- ¼ teaspoon cayenne pepper (optional, for heat)
- 1 can (14 ounces) diced tomatoes
- 2 cups cooked chickpeas (or 1 can, drained and rinsed)
- 1 cup vegetable broth
- 1 cup diced carrots
- 1 cup diced potatoes
- ½ cup chopped dried apricots
- ¼ cup chopped fresh cilantro (plus more for garnish)
- Salt and pepper to taste

INSTRUCTIONS:

a) In a large pot or tagine, heat the olive oil over medium heat. Add the diced onion and minced garlic, and sauté until the onion becomes translucent and fragrant.

b) Add the ground cumin, ground coriander, ground cinnamon, ground ginger, and cayenne pepper (if using) to the pot. Stir well to coat the onion and garlic with the spices.

c) Pour in the diced tomatoes (with their juices) and stir to combine with the spices.

d) Add the cooked chickpeas, vegetable broth, diced carrots, diced potatoes, and chopped dried apricots to the pot. Stir to incorporate all the ingredients.

e) Bring the mixture to a boil, then reduce the heat to low. Cover the pot and simmer for about 45 minutes to 1 hour, or until the vegetables are tender and the flavors have melded together.

f) Stir in the chopped fresh cilantro and season with salt and pepper to taste.

g) Simmer the tagine for an additional 5 minutes to allow the flavors to blend.

h) Serve the Moroccan Chickpea Tagine in bowls, garnished with additional chopped fresh cilantro.

55. Nohutlu Pilav

INGREDIENTS:
- 1 cup chickpeas
- 2 cups short-grain rice
- Hot water to cover the rice
- 1 teaspoon salt
- 3 cups chicken stock
- 4 tablespoons butter
- Salt to taste
- Pepper to taste

INSTRUCTIONS:
a) Place chickpeas in a pan and cover with cold water. Soak overnight.
b) Next day, drain the water and re-cover the chickpeas with water. Place on stove, bring to a boil, then reduce heat to simmer and cook the chickpeas until tender. Set aside to cool. Drain the chickpeas and remove the skins with your fingers as much as possible.
c) Soak the rice in hot but not boiling water with one teaspoon of salt. When cool, drain and rinse under cold water until the water runs clear.
d) Bring the stock to the boil, add the chickpeas and butter. When boiling, stir in the rice and one teaspoon salt. Cover and turn down the heat to low.
e) Let simmer until all the liquid is absorbed by the rice, about 20 minutes. Small holes will appear on the surface of the rice when the liquid is absorbed.
f) Remove from the heat and place a few layers of paper towel under the lid and cover again. Set aside about 10-15 minutes. Before serving, mix gently to fluff the rice. Sprinkle with black pepper if desired.

56. Vegan Chickpea Enchiladas

INGREDIENTS:
- 2 cans (15 oz each) chickpeas, drained and rinsed
- 1 onion, chopped
- 2 cloves garlic, minced
- 1 can (10 oz) red enchilada sauce
- 8-10 corn tortillas
- 1 cup vegan shredded cheddar cheese
- Salt and pepper, to taste

INSTRUCTIONS:
a) Preheat oven to 350°F.
b) In a large skillet, cook the onion and garlic over medium heat until tender.
c) Add the chickpeas to the skillet and stir to combine.
d) Stir in the red enchilada sauce, and season with salt and pepper to taste.
e) Spread a small amount of the chickpea mixture onto each tortilla and roll up tightly.
f) Place the rolled-up tortillas seam-side down in a 9x13 inch baking dish.
g) Sprinkle with vegan shredded cheese and bake for 20-25 minutes, until cheese is melted and bubbly.

57. Socca with Caramelized Onions and Rosemary

INGREDIENTS:
SOCCA
- 1½ cups water
- 1⅓ cups (6 ounces) chickpea flour
- ¼ cup extra-virgin olive oil, divided
- 1 teaspoon table salt
- ¼ teaspoon ground cumin

TOPPING
- 2 tablespoons extra-virgin olive oil, plus extra for drizzling
- 2 cups thinly sliced onions
- ½ teaspoon table salt
- 1 teaspoon chopped fresh rosemary
- Coarse sea salt

INSTRUCTIONS:
FOR THE SOCCA
a) Adjust oven rack to middle position and heat oven to 200 degrees. Set wire rack in rimmed baking sheet and place in oven to preheat. Whisk water, flour, 4 teaspoons oil, salt, and cumin in bowl until no lumps remain. Let batter rest while preparing topping, at least 10 minutes.

FOR THE TOPPING
b) Heat oil in 10-inch nonstick skillet over medium-high heat until just smoking.

c) Add onions and salt and cook until onions start to brown around edges but still have some texture, 7 to 10 minutes.

d) Add rosemary and cook until fragrant, about 1 minute. Transfer onion mixture to bowl; set aside. Wipe skillet clean with paper towels.

e) Heat 2 teaspoons oil in now-empty skillet over medium-high heat until just smoking.

f) Lift skillet off heat and pour $\frac{1}{2}$ cup batter into far side of skillet; swirl gently in clockwise direction until batter evenly covers bottom of skillet.
g) Return skillet to heat and cook socca, without moving it, until well browned and crisp around bottom edge, 3 to 4 minutes (you can peek at underside of socca by loosening it from side of skillet with heat resistant rubber spatula).
h) Flip socca with rubber spatula and cook until second side is just cooked, about 1 minute.
i) Transfer socca, browned side up, to prepared wire rack in oven. Repeat 3 more times, using 2 teaspoons oil and $\frac{1}{2}$ cup batter per batch.
j) Transfer socca to cutting board and cut each into wedges. Serve, topped with sautéed onions, drizzled with extra oil, and sprinkled with sea salt.

58. Basmati & Wild Rice with Chickpeas, Currants & Herbs

INGREDIENTS:
- ⅓ cup / 50 g wild rice
- 2½ tbsp olive oil
- rounded 1 cup / 220 g basmati rice
- 1½ cups / 330 ml boiling water
- 2 tsp cumin seeds
- 1½ tsp curry powder
- 1½ cups / 240 g cooked and drained chickpeas (canned are fine)
- ¾ cup / 180 ml sunflower oil
- 1 medium onion, thinly sliced
- 1½ tsp all-purpose flour
- ⅔ cup / 100 g currants
- 2 tbsp chopped flat-leaf parsley
- 1 tbsp chopped cilantro
- 1 tbsp chopped dill
- salt and freshly ground black pepper

INSTRUCTIONS

i) Start by putting the wild rice in a small saucepan, cover with plenty of water, bring to a boil, and leave to simmer for about 40 minutes, until the rice is cooked but still quite firm. Drain and set aside.

j) To cook the basmati rice, pour 1 tablespoon of the olive oil into a medium saucepan with a tightly fitting lid and place over high heat. Add the rice and ¼ teaspoon salt and stir as you warm up the rice. Carefully add the boiling water, decrease the heat to very low, cover the pan with the lid, and leave to cook for 15 minutes.

k) Remove the pan from the heat, cover with a clean tea towel and then the lid, and leave off the heat for 10 minutes.

l) While the rice is cooking, prepare the chickpeas. Heat the remaining 1½ tbsp olive oil in a small saucepan over high heat. Add the cumin seeds and curry powder, wait for a couple seconds, and then add the chickpeas and ¼ teaspoon salt; make sure you do this quickly or the spices may burn in the oil. Stir over the heat for a minute or two, just to heat the chickpeas, then transfer to a large mixing bowl.

m) Wipe the saucepan clean, pour in the sunflower oil, and place over high heat. Make sure the oil is hot by throwing in a small piece of onion; it should sizzle vigorously. Use your hands to mix the onion with the flour to coat it slightly. Take some of the onion and carefully (it may spit!) place it in the oil. Fry for 2 to 3 minutes, until golden brown, then transfer to paper towels to drain and sprinkle with salt. Repeat in batches until all the onion is fried.

n) Finally, add both types of rice to the chickpeas and then add the currants, herbs, and fried onion. Stir, taste, and add salt and pepper as you like. Serve warm or at room temperature.

SOUPS AND CURRY

59. Mexican Margarita Chickpea Soup

INGREDIENTS:
- ½ cup diced red pepper
- ½ cup diced green pepper
- ½ cup diced sweet onion
- 3 cloves garlic chopped
- ½ cup tequila make sure it's vegan to keep this vegan
- 1 tablespoon fresh lime juice
- 2 tablespoons chopped fresh cilantro
- 1 tablespoon cumin Simply Organic brand
- ¼ teaspoon coriander Simply Organic brand
- ¼ teaspoon chipotle powder
- 1 ½ teaspoons Himalayan pink salt divided
- 1 ½ cups dried chickpeas soaked overnight
- 6 cups veggie broth plus some to sauté

OPTIONAL TOPPINGS:
- Corn tortillas sliced into thin strips
- Avocado chopped
- Fresh cilantro
- Fresh lime juice

INSTRUCTIONS:
a) Preheat oven to 300°F if using a Dutch oven.

b) Sauté peppers, onions, and garlic over medium heat until just soft with only ½ teaspoon of the salt, and use broth to sauté until they just begin to get soft.

c) Add tequila, lime juice, and cilantro. Cook until the liquid is reduced by half, it took me about 7-10 minutes.

d) Add spices, the rest of the salt, and the pre-soaked chickpeas and mix for about a minute. Then add the broth.

e) Bring it to a simmer, then if using the Dutch oven, cover it and put it in the preheated oven and allow it to slowly cook for 45-60 minutes. Check at 45 minutes and if the chickpeas aren't soft yet allow them to cook longer. You can leave it up to 60 minutes to allow it to gain more flavor.

f) If you are using a regular soup pot, then once the soup starts simmering, turn the heat to low and allow it to slowly cook, covered, for 30-60 minutes.

g) Once the soup is done, put tortilla strips in a bowl then pour soup over the top so they can soak and get soft.

h) Top with fresh toppings of choice and enjoy.

60. Chickpea, Pumpkin, and Coconut Curry

INGREDIENTS:
- 2 tablespoons coconut butter
- ½ cup onion, diced
- 3 cloves garlic, minced
- 1 tablespoon ginger, grated
- 2½ cups pumpkin, peeled and cubed
- 2½ tablespoons red curry paste
- 14-ounce can of coconut milk
- 2 cups broccoli, cut into florets
- 1 cup canned chickpeas
- ½ cup cashews, unsalted
- 1 tablespoon lime juice
- ¼ cup cilantro, chopped

INSTRUCTIONS:
a) Heat the coconut butter for 1 minute.
b) Add the onion, ginger, and garlic, and sauté for 2 minutes, or until the onions are tender, transparent, and fragrant.
c) Add the curry paste and pumpkin. Cook for 1 minute more.
d) Bring the mixture to a boil while stirring in the coconut milk.
e) Cover and reduce the heat to low. Simmer for 15 minutes.
f) Add the broccoli and cook for another 5 minutes, uncovered.
g) Add the chickpeas, cashews, and lime juice, and cook for another 4 minutes.
h) Before serving, garnish with cilantro.

61. Chickpea curry with sea moss

INGREDIENTS:
- 2 cups butternut squash, diced
- 2 cups of kale, chopped
- 1 cup cooked chickpeas
- 2 Tablespoons coconut or grapeseed oil
- 1 medium onion, finely chopped
- 1 plum tomato, diced
- 2 large cloves of garlic
- ½ can coconut milk + 1 cup water
- 2 teaspoons curry spice blend
- 2 - 3 Tablespoons of plain sea moss gel
- 1 teaspoons salt
- 1 Tablespoon lime juice
- 2 Tablespoons cilantro, chopped plus more for garnish
- cayenne pepper or red pepper flakes

INSTRUCTIONS:
a) Cook jasmine rice 2 cups rice, 3 cups water, and salt until soft and water are absorbed.
b) Heat oil and cook onions until translucent.
c) Add garlic, tomato, salt, curry blend, and pepper. cook for about 3 minutes.
d) Add butternut and chickpeas and stir until coated with seasoning.
e) Add coconut milk and water. stir to combine well. cover and simmer for 15 minutes until squash is cooked. stirring occasionally. add water if needed.
f) Add kale, cilantro, sea moss gel, lime juice, and salt. cook for about 10 more minutes until the kale is wilted, but not overcooked.
g) Serve in your favorite bowl, and top with cilantro and a squeeze of lime juice.

62. Chickpea Mushroom Soup

INGREDIENTS:

- 2 pcs Ashwagandha roots
- 4 pcs Red dates, pitted
- 4 pcs Dried/ fresh almond mushrooms
- $\frac{1}{2}$ cup Chickpeas, soaked
- 7 cups Water
- Salt To taste

INSTRUCTIONS:

a) Wash and chop the fresh mushrooms. If you use dried mushrooms, soak them in water for 15 minutes. Then cut it into pieces.
b) Soak chickpeas in water for at least 2 hours. Then, drain the water and keep it aside.
c) Next, put all the ingredients in a pot. Turn the stove on and bring it to a boil.
d) Simmer the soup on medium to low heat for 45 minutes.
e) Add salt and stir well.
f) Pour the soup into bowls. Serve hot.

63. Curried Chickpea Meatballs

INGREDIENTS:
- 3 tablespoons olive oil
- 1 onion, chopped
- 1½ teaspoons hot or mild curry powder
- ½ teaspoon salt
- 1/8 teaspoon ground cayenne
- 1 cup cooked chickpeas
- 1 tablespoon chopped fresh parsley
- ½ cup wheat gluten flour
- 1/3 cup dry unseasoned almond flour

INSTRUCTIONS:
a) In a skillet, heat 1 tablespoon of the oil over moderate heat.
b) Add the onion, cover, and cook until softened, 5 minutes. Stir in 1 teaspoon of the curry powder, salt, and cayenne and remove from the heat. Set aside.
c) In a food processor, combine the chickpeas, parsley, wheat gluten flour, almond flour, and cooked onion.
d) Form the chickpea mixture into 4 equal Meatballs and set aside.
e) In a skillet, heat the remaining 2 tablespoons of oil over moderate heat.
f) Add the Meatballs, cover, and cook until golden brown on both sides, turning once, about 5 minutes per side.
g) In a bowl, combine the remaining ½ teaspoon of curry powder with the mayonnaise, stirring to blend.

64. Tortellini Soup

INGREDIENTS:
- 1 carrot, peeled and grated
- 1 onion, grated
- 2 cloves garlic, minced
- 2 tablespoons olive oil
- 15-ounce can no salt added diced tomatoes
- 15-ounce can of low-sodium chickpeas, drained
- 3 cups reduced-sodium chicken broth
- 1 9-ounce package of refrigerated three-cheese tortellini
- 1 teaspoon dried Italian herb blend
- 2 cups lightly packed fresh baby spinach
- Shaved Parmesan cheese for serving

INSTRUCTIONS:
a) Combine the carrot, onion, garlic, and olive oil in a 3-qt. microwave-safe bowl.
b) Microwave, uncovered, on high heat for 3 minutes.
c) Stir in the chicken broth, tomatoes, chickpeas, tortellini, and Italian herb blend.
d) Cover the bowl tightly with a glass lid or plastic wrap and cook for 8 minutes on high.
e) Remove the bowl from the microwave, carefully uncover it, and stir in the spinach.
f) Let stand for 1 or 2 minutes to allow the spinach to wilt.
g) Serve with Parmesan cheese, if desired.

65. Spinach and beet soup

INGREDIENTS:

- ½ cup Chickpeas
- 2 cups Spinach; chopped
- 1 cup Kidney beans
- 1 cup Fresh dill weed -or-
- ¼ cup Dried dill weed
- 1 cup Lentils
- 4 Beets; peeled & cubed small
- 1 large Onion; chopped (up to)
- 2 tablespoons Flour (up to)
- 2 Soup bones; optional
- Fried onions & dry mint leaves (for garnish)
- Salt & pepper to taste
- Oil for frying (up to)
- 8 cups Water

INSTRUCTIONS:

a) Soak the chickpeas & kidney beans for 2 hours or overnight. Cook the lentils in 1-2 cups of water till soft but not mushy & set aside.

b) Brown the bones and onions in oil in a large kettle. Season to taste and add water, chickpeas, kidney beans, & beets. Cook until the chickpeas are soft.

c) Remove bones & add spinach, dill weed, and lentils. Stir occasionally. Meanwhile, brown flour in a little bit of oil and add to the soup to thicken it.

d) Put the soup on low heat & stir frequently until done. Serve in a bowl & garnish with fried onion or with dried mint leaves added to hot oil.

66. Moroccan Chickpea Stew

INGREDIENTS:
- 1 tablespoon olive oil
- 1 onion, diced
- 2 cloves garlic, minced
- 1 carrot, diced
- 1 red bell pepper, diced
- 1 teaspoon ground cumin
- 1 teaspoon ground coriander
- $\frac{1}{2}$ teaspoon ground turmeric
- $\frac{1}{2}$ teaspoon ground cinnamon
- 1 can (14 ounces) diced tomatoes
- 2 cups cooked chickpeas (or 1 can, rinsed and drained)
- 2 cups low-sodium vegetable broth
- Salt and pepper to taste
- Fresh cilantro or parsley, chopped, for garnish

INSTRUCTIONS:
a) In a large pot, heat the olive oil over medium heat. Add the onion, garlic, carrot, and red bell pepper. Cook until the vegetables are softened.

b) Add the cumin, coriander, turmeric, and cinnamon to the pot. Stir well to coat the vegetables with the spices.

c) Pour in the diced tomatoes, chickpeas, and vegetable broth. Season with salt and pepper to taste.

d) Bring the stew to a boil, then reduce the heat and simmer for 15-20 minutes to allow the flavors to meld together.

e) Serve the Moroccan chickpea stew garnished with fresh cilantro or parsley.

67. Indian Chickpea Curry

INGREDIENTS:
- 2 tablespoons vegetable oil
- 1 onion, diced
- 2 cloves garlic, minced
- 1 tablespoon grated ginger
- 1 teaspoon ground cumin
- 1 teaspoon ground coriander
- ½ teaspoon turmeric
- ½ teaspoon paprika
- ¼ teaspoon cayenne pepper (adjust to taste)
- 1 can (14 ounces) diced tomatoes
- 2 cans (14 ounces each) chickpeas, rinsed and drained
- ½ cup water
- Salt to taste
- Fresh cilantro, chopped, for garnish

INSTRUCTIONS:
a) Heat the vegetable oil in a large pan over medium heat. Add the onion, garlic, and ginger. Cook until the onion is translucent.

b) Add the ground cumin, ground coriander, turmeric, paprika, and cayenne pepper to the pan. Stir well to coat the onions and spices.

c) Pour in the diced tomatoes, chickpeas, and water. Season with salt to taste.

d) Bring the mixture to a simmer and cook for 15-20 minutes, allowing the flavors to meld together and the sauce to thicken slightly.

e) Serve the Indian chickpea curry hot, garnished with fresh cilantro. It pairs well with rice or naan bread.

68.Chickpea Sweet Potato Stew

INGREDIENTS:
- 15oz chickpeas, drained and rinsed
- 2 cups sweet potato, peeled and diced
- 4 tablespoons vegetable broth
- 15oz fire-roasted crushed tomato, 1 can
- 3 cloves garlic, minced
- 1 small onion, diced
- 1 teaspoon ginger, minced
- 3 cups vegetable broth
- 5oz fresh spinach
- 1/4 teaspoon dried coriander
- 1/8 teaspoon cayenne
- 1 tablespoon sweet paprika
- 1/2 teaspoon cumin

INSTRUCTIONS:
a) In a large pot or oven, heat the vegetable broth over medium heat. Once the broth simmers, cook the onion for 4-5 minutes or until it is translucent.

b) Stir in the garlic and ginger for at least 2 to 3 minutes. Cook and stir it occasionally until fragrant, then add sweet paprika, cumin, coriander, and cayenne.

c) Bring the chickpeas, sweet potatoes, crushed tomatoes, and vegetable broth to a boil in a saucepan. Reduce heat to medium-low and let the sweet potatoes cook for 15-20 minutes, or until tender.

d) Stir in the spinach until it is softened. Serve immediately.

69. Chickpea & Farro Stew

INGREDIENTS:
- 3 cups cooked chickpeas
- 1/2 cup pearled farro
- 1 medium carrot, diced
- 14.5oz tomato can, diced
- 2 cloves garlic, minced
- 3 1/2 cups vegetable broth
- 4 tablespoons vegetable broth
- 1 sprig rosemary
- 1 medium onion, diced
- 1 rib celery, diced
- 1/4 teaspoon freshly ground black pepper
- 1/2 teaspoon salt
- 1/3 cup freshly grated plant-based cheese
- 2 cups lightly packed baby spinach leaves, coarsely chopped

INSTRUCTIONS:
a) In a blender, combine 1 cup chickpeas and $\frac{1}{2}$ cup vegetable broth to make a smooth puree.

b) In a saucepot, heat the vegetable broth over medium heat. When the broth simmers, add the onion, carrot, and celery. Cook for 6 to 8 minutes, occasionally stirring until the vegetables are soft.

c) Cook the garlic for a minute. After that, add the remaining 2 cups of chickpeas, the remaining 3 cups of broth, the tomatoes and their juices, the rosemary, salt, and pepper. Stir them to combine.

d) Boil, then reduce to a medium-low setting and cook for 15 minutes.

e) Increase the heat to medium-high and add the farro.

f) Allow the soup to boil, then reduce the heat to medium-low and cook. Stir occasionally for at least 20 minutes or until the farro is tender.

g) Remove the rosemary sprig and stir in the spinach. Cook more for at least 1 to 2 minutes, then add in the chickpea puree. Serve immediately.

70. Curry Chana Stew From Trinidad

INGREDIENTS:
- 4 cups chickpeas, soaked overnight
- 1 serrano chile pepper, seeded, and minced
- 3 teaspoon curry powder
- 1 tablespoon olive oil
- 1 yellow onion
- $\frac{1}{4}$ teaspoon methi/fenugreek
- $1\frac{1}{4}$ cups water, divided
- 3 garlic cloves, minced
- $\frac{1}{2}$ teaspoon turmeric
- $\frac{1}{2}$ teaspoon cumin
- $\frac{1}{2}$ teaspoon salt
- 2 tablespoons cilantro, chopped

INSTRUCTIONS:
a) Boil the chickpeas in water for $1\frac{1}{2}$ hours, or until they are soft.
a) Drain the beans while saving the cooking liquid.
b) In a pot over medium-high heat, heat the olive oil.
c) Add the onion slices and cook for 5 minutes, or until transparent.
d) Add the serrano chile and garlic, cooking for a further 2 to 3 minutes, or until aromatic.
e) Stir in the curry powder, cumin, turmeric, and methi for about 30 seconds.
f) Pour in $\frac{1}{4}$ cup of water, chickpea cooking liquid, or broth while stirring the mixture.
g) Add the cooked chickpeas, and simmer for 5 minutes on low heat.
h) Remove the lid from the pot, add the salt and continue to simmer for another 20 minutes.
i) Top with the cilantro, and serve with brown rice.

71. Cauliflower soup with pomegranate

INGREDIENTS:
- 3 medium carrots, roughly chopped
- 3 medium celery stalks, roughly chopped
- 3 onions, roughly chopped
- 3 medium leeks, roughly chopped
- 700g potatoes, peeled and roughly chopped
- 3 tablespoons olive oil
- 1 head of garlic, roughly chopped
- 3 bay leaves
- 2 tablespoons dark muscovado sugar
- 1 large cauliflower, roughly chopped
- 2 x 440g tins chickpeas
- 3-4 liters of vegetable stock
- 1 tablespoon harissa
- A small bunch of parsley
- Juice of 1 lemon
- Salt and black pepper

SPICES:
- 2 tablespoons cumin
- 1 tablespoon ground coriander
- 1 tablespoon paprika
- 1 tablespoon smoked paprika
- 1 teaspoon chili flakes
- 1 teaspoon ground cinnamon
- 1 teaspoon ground nutmeg

TO SERVE
- Seeds of 1 pomegranate
- Pomegranate molasses

- 1 small bunch of fresh coriander

INSTRUCTIONS:

a) Fry the carrot, celery, white onion, leek, and potato in the olive oil until they have a little color. Add the garlic, bay, spices, and sugar and sweat until the spices release their aroma.

b) Remove and discard the leaves and hard stalk of the cauliflower, then roughly chop the edible parts and add them to the soup base. Add the chickpeas, vegetable stock, and harissa paste, if using, and cook until all the vegetables are tender: about 20 minutes.

c) Add the parsley and lemon juice and, using a hand blender or food processor, blitz the soup until rich and smooth. You may need to add a little more stock if it's too thick. Taste and season with salt and pepper.

d) To serve, ladle into a bowl and decorate with a sprinkle of pomegranate seeds, a few drops of pomegranate molasses, and picked coriander leaves.

72. Watercress & chickpea soup with rose water

INGREDIENTS:

- 2 medium carrots (9 oz / 250 g in total), cut into ¾-inch / 2cm dice
- 3 tbsp olive oil
- 2½ tsp ras el hanout
- ½ tsp ground cinnamon
- 1½ cups / 240 g cooked chickpeas, fresh or canned
- 1 medium onion, thinly sliced
- 2½ tbsp / 15 g peeled and finely chopped fresh ginger
- 2½ cups / 600 ml vegetable stock
- 7 oz / 200 g watercress
- 3½ oz / 100 g spinach leaves
- 2 tsp superfine sugar
- 1 tsp rose water
- salt
- Greek yogurt, to serve (optional)
- Preheat the oven to 425°F / 220°C.

INSTRUCTIONS:

a) Mix the carrots with 1 tablespoon of the olive oil, the ras el hanout, cinnamon, and a generous pinch of salt and spread flat in a roasting pan lined with parchment paper. Place in the oven for 15 minutes, then add half the chickpeas, stir well, and cook for another 10 minutes, until the carrot softens but still has a bite.

b) Meanwhile, place the onion and ginger in a large saucepan. Sauté with the remaining olive oil for about 10 minutes over medium heat, until the onion is completely soft and golden. Add the remaining chickpeas, stock, watercress, spinach, sugar, and ¾ teaspoon salt, stir well, and bring to a boil. Cook for a minute or two, just until the leaves wilt.

c) Using a food processor or blender, blitz the soup until smooth. Add the rose water, stir, taste, and add more salt

or rose water if you like. Set aside until the carrot and chickpeas are ready, then reheat to serve.
d) To serve, divide the soup among four bowls and top with the hot carrot and chickpeas and, if you like, about 2 teaspoons yogurt per portion.

SALADS

73. Canned Chickpea and Tofu Cheese Salad

INGREDIENTS:
SALAD:
- 1 large cucumber, chopped
- Two 15-ounce cans of chickpeas, rinsed and drained
- ½ cup chopped red onion
- ¼ cup minced basil
- ¼ cup cherry tomatoes halved (optional)

TOFU CHEESE
- 10 ounces of firm tofu, pressed, and cubed
- ¼ cup of lemon juice
- ½ cup of water
- ½ cup of apple cider vinegar
- 1 tbsp of oregano

DRESSING:
- 4 Tablespoons fresh lemon juice
- 1¼ cup white balsamic vinegar
- 1½ teaspoons Dijon mustard
- 2 garlic cloves, minced
- 1 teaspoon dried parsley
- Salt and black pepper to taste

INSTRUCTIONS:
FOR THE TOFU CHEESE
a) Combine the lemon juice, apple cider vinegar, water, and oregano in a bowl.
b) Place the tofu cubes into the marinade, and marinate for at least4 hours.

FOR THE SALAD
c) Mix all salad ingredients, along with the tofu cheese, in a bowl and set aside.

FOR THE DRESSING
d) Add all dressing ingredients to a bowl and whisk until well mixed.

e) Drizzle over salad and toss well.

74. Loaded Greens and Seeds Salad

INGREDIENTS:
- 3½ ounces tofu
- 1 Handful of rocket eaves
- 1 bunch of cos lettuce
- 1 Handful of lamb's lettuce
- 2 bunches of baby spinach
- ½ can of chickpeas
- 1 avocado
- 1 handful of seeds & nuts
- 6 cherry tomatoes
- ½ cucumber
- 1 serving of quinoa, cooked
- ½ green or red pepper
- Olive oil
- Lemon
- Himalayan salt & black pepper

INSTRUCTIONS:
a) Fry the tofu lightly in almond oil.
b) Toss everything together.

75. Couscous & Chick-Pea Salad

INGREDIENTS:
- 1 cup couscous
- 1 can chickpeas, drained and rinsed
- 1 cup cherry tomatoes, halved
- ½ cup cucumber, diced
- ¼ cup red onion, finely chopped
- ¼ cup fresh parsley, chopped
- 2 tablespoons olive oil
- 2 tablespoons lemon juice
- Salt and pepper to taste

INSTRUCTIONS:
a) Cook the couscous according to the package instructions. Fluff with a fork and et it cool.
b) In a large bowl, combine the cooked couscous, chickpeas, cherry tomatoes, cucumber, red onion, and parsley.
c) In a small bowl, whisk together the olive oil, lemon juice, salt, and pepper.
d) Pour the dressing over the couscous mixture and toss to coat everything evenly.
e) Taste and adjust the seasoning if needed.
f) Pack the salad in a lunchbox, and it's ready to go.

76. Cauliflower & Chickpeas Salad

INGREDIENTS:

- 3/4 cup dried chickpeas, rinsed and drained
- 2 tbsp curry powder
- 1 medium cauliflower head, cut into florets
- 1 1/2 cups vegetable broth
- 2 garlic cloves, minced
- 2 tbsp ginger, minced
- 1 bell pepper, chopped
- 1 onion, chopped
- 2 tsp olive oil
- 3 cups water
- 1/4 tsp salt

INSTRUCTIONS:

a) Add chickpeas and water into the instant pot.
b) Seal pot with lid and cook on high for 45 minutes.
c) Allow to release pressure naturally for 15 minutes then release using quick release method.
d) Drain chickpeas well and place in a bowl.
e) Add oil into the instant pot and set the pot on sauté mode.
f) Add onion and sauté for 3 minutes.
g) Add bell pepper and sauté for 3 minutes.
h) Add garlic and ginger and sauté for 30 seconds.
i) Add cauliflower, broth, chickpeas, curry powder, and salt. Stir well.
j) Seal pot with lid and cook on high for 3 minutes.
k) Release pressure using quick release method than open the lid.
l) Serve and enjoy.

77. Smoky chickpea tuna salad

INGREDIENTS:
CHICKPEA TUNA:
- 15 oz. of cooked chickpeas canned or otherwise.
- 2-3 Tablespoons non-dairy plain yogurt or vegan mayo.
- 2 teaspoons Dijon mustard.
- 1/2 teaspoons ground cumin.
- 1/2 teaspoons smoked paprika.
- 1 Tablespoons fresh lemon juice.
- 1 celery stalk diced.
- 2 scallions chopped.
- Sea salt to taste.

SANDWICH ASSEMBLY:
- 4 pieces of rye bread or sprouted wheat bread.
- 1 cup infant spinach.
- 1 avocado sliced or cubed.
- Salt + pepper.

INSTRUCTIONS:
a) Prepare the chickpea tuna salad

b) In a food processor, pulse the chickpeas till they resemble a coarse, crumbly texture. Spoon the chickpeas into a medium-sized bowl and include the remainder of the active ingredients, stirring till well combined. Season with plenty of sea salt to your own taste.

c) Make your sandwich

d) Layer the baby spinach on each slice of bread; add several heaping of chickpea tuna salad, spreading out evenly. Top with avocado slices, a couple of grains of sea salt, and newly ground pepper.

78. Spiced Chickpeas & Vegetable Salad

INGREDIENTS:
- ½ cup / 100 g dried chickpeas
- 1 tsp baking soda
- 2 small cucumbers (10 oz / 280 g in total)
- 2 large tomatoes (10½ oz / 300 g in total)
- 8½ oz / 240 g radishes
- 1 red pepper, seeded and ribs removed
- 1 small red onion, peeled
- ⅔ oz / 20 g cilantro leaves and stems, coarsely chopped
- ½ oz / 15 g flat-leaf parsley, coarsely chopped
- 6 tbsp / 90 ml olive oil
- grated zest of 1 lemon, plus 2 tbsp juice
- 1½ tbsp sherry vinegar
- 1 clove garlic, crushed
- 1 tsp superfine sugar
- 1 tsp ground cardamom
- 1½ tsp ground allspice
- 1 tsp ground cumin
- Greek yogurt (optional)
- salt and freshly ground black pepper

INSTRUCTIONS:
a) Soak the dried chickpeas overnight in a large bowl with plenty of cold water and the baking soda. The next day, drain, place in a large saucepan, and cover with water twice the volume of the chickpeas. Bring to a boil and simmer, skimming off any foam, for about an hour, until completely tender, then drain.

b) Cut the cucumber, tomato, radish, and pepper into ⅔-inch / 1.5cm dice; cut the onion into ¼-inch / 0.5cm dice. Mix everything together in a bowl with the cilantro and parsley.

c) In a jar or sealable container, mix 5 tbsp / 75 ml of the olive oil, the lemon juice and zest, vinegar, garlic, and sugar and mix well to form a dressing, then season to taste with salt and pepper. Pour the dressing over the salad and toss lightly.

d) Mix together the cardamom, allspice, cumin, and ¼ teaspoon salt and spread on a plate. Toss the cooked chickpeas in the spice mixture in a few batches to coat well. Heat the remaining olive oil in a frying pan over medium heat and lightly fry the chickpeas for 2 to 3 minutes, gently shaking the pan so they cook evenly and don't stick. Keep warm.

e) Divide the salad among four plates, arranging it in a large circle, and spoon the warm spiced chickpeas on top, keeping the edge of the salad clear. You can drizzle some Greek yogurt on top to make the salad creamy.

BUDDHA BOWLS

79. Chickpea Bowl

INGREDIENTS:
- 1/2 cup dried chickpeas; rinsed, soaked and drained
- 1/2 tbsp. olive oil
- 1/2 onion; chopped.
- 1/2 tbsp. fresh ginger; minced
- 1/2 tbsp. garlic; minced
- 1/2 tsp. ground coriander
- 1 medium tomato; chopped finely
- 1/2 tsp. curry powder
- 1/2 tsp. ground cumin
- 1/2 cup water
- Pinch of salt
- Freshly ground black pepper to taste
- 1 tbsp. fresh parsley; chopped.

INSTRUCTIONS:
a) Add oil and onion to Instant Pot and Select the *Sauté* function to cook for 3 minutes.
b) Now add the garlic, ginger and spices to cook for another 2 minutes
c) Add water and chickpeas to the pot then secure the lid
d) Switch the cooker to the Manual function with high pressure and 20 minutes cooking time
e) When it is done; do a Quick release then remove the lid
f) Sprinkle some salt and black pepper on top and garnish with parsley. Serve hot

80. Scrambled Chickpea Breakfast Bowls

INGREDIENTS:
- 2 packed cups (60 g) baby spinach
- 3 tablespoons (45 ml) avocado or extra-virgin olive oil, divided
- 8 ounces (225 g) riced cauliflower
- Kosher salt and freshly ground black pepper
- ½ medium onion, diced
- 1 red bell pepper, cored and diced 3 cups (600 g) or 2 (15-ounce, or 420 g) cans chickpeas, drained and rinsed
- 1 clove garlic, minced
- 2 teaspoons (4 g) ground cumin
- 1 teaspoon (2 g) ground coriander
- 1 teaspoon (2 g) turmeric
- 2 avocados, peeled, pitted, and thinly sliced
- 1 recipe Green Tahini Sauce (page 26)

INSTRUCTIONS

a) Divide the spinach among bowls.

b) Heat 1 tablespoon (15 ml) of the oil in a large, high-sided skillet over medium heat. Add the riced cauliflower and season with salt and pepper. Cook, stirring occasionally, until tender, about 3 minutes. Spoon over the spinach.

c) Heat the remaining 2 tablespoons (30 ml) oil in the same skillet over medium heat. Add the onion, bell pepper, salt, and pepper. Cook, stirring occasionally, until soft and fragrant, about 5 minutes. Meanwhile, mash half of the chickpeas with a fork. Stir in the whole and mashed chickpeas, garlic, cumin, coriander, and turmeric, and cook, stirring occasionally until soft, about 3 minutes.

d) To serve, top the spinach and riced cauliflower with the chick-peas and avocado. Drizzle with Green Tahini Sauce.

81. Za'atar Chickpea Bowls

INGREDIENTS:
- 4 medium carrots
- 3 tablespoons (45 ml) avocado or extra-virgin olive oil, divided
- Kosher salt and freshly ground black pepper
- 1 cup (175 g) quinoa, rinsed
- 2 cups (470 ml) water
- 2 teaspoons (10 ml) apple cider vinegar
- 6 cups (420 g) shredded kale, divided
- ½ yellow onion, diced
- 1½ cups (300 g) or 1 (15-ounce, or 420 g) can chickpeas, drained and rinsed
- 2 teaspoons (4 g) za'atar
- 1 teaspoon (2 g) ground cumin
- 2 beets, peeled and thinly sliced
- ¾ cup (180 ml) Cilantro Yogurt Sauce
- Sesame seeds

INSTRUCTIONS

a) Preheat the oven to 400°F (200°C, or gas mark 6).

b) Peel and cut the carrots into ¼-inch (6 mm)-thick slices. Toss with 1 tablespoon (15 ml) of the oil, salt, and pepper, and arrange in a single layer on a rimmed baking sheet. Roast until tender and browned around the edges, about 20 minutes, flipping over halfway through.

c) Meanwhile, combine the quinoa, water, and a pinch of salt in a medium saucepan. Bring to a boil, then reduce the heat to low, cover, and simmer until tender, about 15 minutes. Remove from the heat, stir in the vinegar and 2 cups (140 g) of the kale, and steam with the lid on for about 5 minutes.

d) Meanwhile, heat the remaining 2 tablespoons (30 ml) oil in a large skillet over medium heat. Add the onion and cook, stirring occasionally, until soft. Stir in the chickpeas, za'atar, cumin, salt, and pepper. Cook, stirring occasionally, until the chickpeas are heated through and fragrant, about 5 minutes.

e) To serve, divide the quinoa among bowls. Top with chickpeas, carrots, the remaining 4 cups (280 g) kale, and sliced beets. Drizzle with Cilantro Yogurt Sauce and sprinkle with sesame seeds.

82. Cauliflower Falafel Power Bowls

INGREDIENTS:
- 3 cups or 2 (15-ounce, or 420 g) cans chickpeas, drained and rinsed
- 1 small red onion, roughly chopped
- 2 cloves garlic
- 2 tablespoons (30 ml) freshly squeezed lemon juice
- ½ packed cup (24 g) fresh parsley leaves
- ½ packed cup (8 g) fresh cilantro leaves
- 2 teaspoons (4 g) ground cumin
- 1 teaspoon (2 g) ground coriander
- $^1/_8$ teaspoon cayenne pepper
- Kosher salt and freshly ground black pepper
- 3 tablespoons (24 g) all-purpose flour
- 1 teaspoon (5 g) baking powder
- 1 tablespoon (15 ml) avocado or extra-virgin olive oil
- 16 ounces (455 g) riced cauliflower
- 2 teaspoons (4 g) za'atar
- 2 packed cups (40 g) arugula
- 1 medium red bell pepper, cored and chopped
- 2 avocados, peeled, pitted, and diced
- Red cabbage or beet sauerkraut
- Hummus

INSTRUCTIONS

a) If using dried beans, add the chickpeas to a medium bowl and cover with water by at least 1 inch (2.5 cm). Let them sit, uncovered, at room temperature for 24 hours.

b) Preheat the oven to 375°F (190°C, or gas mark 5).

c) Add the drained chickpeas, onion, garlic, lemon juice, parsley, cilantro, cumin, coriander, cayenne, 1 teaspoon (6 g) of salt, and ¼ teaspoon pepper to the bowl of a food processor. Pulse about 10 times until the chickpeas are chopped. Scrape down the sides of the bowl, add the flour and baking powder, and pulse until the mixture is well combined.

d) Scoop out about 2 tablespoons of the mixture and roll it into a ball in the palms of your hands. Transfer to a lightly greased baking sheet and use a spatula to flatten into a ½-inch (1.3 cm)-thick disk. Repeat with the remainder of the mixture.

e) Bake the falafel until cooked through and tender, 25 to 30 minutes, flipping once halfway through.

f) Heat the oil in a large skillet over medium heat. Add the riced cauliflower, za'ctar, salt, and pepper, and stir to combine. Cook, stirring occasionally, until the cauliflower is slightly softened, about 3 minutes.

g) To serve, divide the cauliflower rice and arugula among bowls. Top with falafel patties, bell pepper, avocado, sauerkraut, and a scoop of hummus.

83. Herbed Chickpea and Bulgur Bowls

INGREDIENTS:
- 1½ cups (300 g) or 1 (15-ounce, or 420 g) can chickpeas, drained and rinsed
- 1 tablespoon (15 ml) avocado or extra-virgin olive oil
- ¼ cup (40 g) diced red onion
- 2 tablespoons (6 g) finely chopped parsley
- 1 tablespoon (1 g) finely chopped cilantro
- ½ teaspoon sumac
- Kosher salt and freshly ground black pepper
- ¾ cup (125 g) bulgur
- 1½ cups (355 ml) water
- 2 packed cups (40 g) arugula
- 2 teaspoons (10 ml) apple cider vinegar
- ½ head broccoli, cut into small florets
- 2 cups (140 g) finely shredded red cabbage
- 2 avocados, peeled, pitted, and thinly sliced
- ¾ cup (180 ml) Roasted Red Pepper
- Sauce

INSTRUCTIONS

a) Add the chickpeas, oil, onion, herbs, sumac, salt, and pepper to a medium bowl, and stir to combine. Set aside to marinate while you prepare the remainder of the bowl.

b) Combine the bulgur, water, and a generous pinch of salt in a medium saucepan. Bring to a boil, then cover, reduce the heat to low, and simmer until tender, 10 to 15 minutes. Remove from the heat and stir in the arugula and vinegar.

c) Meanwhile, steam the broccoli.

d) To serve, divide the bulgur and cabbage among bowls. Top with chickpeas, broccoli, avocado, and Roasted Red Pepper Sauce.

84. Butternut Squash and Kale Bowls

INGREDIENTS:
- ½ cup (82 g) pearled farro
- 1¼ cups (295 ml) water
- Kosher salt and freshly ground black pepper
- 1 small butternut squash, peeled and cut into ½-inch (1.3 cm)-thick batons
- 1 pound (455 g) Brussels sprouts, trimmed and halved
- 2 tablespoons (30 ml) avocado, coconut, or extra-virgin olive oil
- 3 cups (360 g) steamed kale
- 1 cup (40 g) shredded radicchio
- 1 firm apple, cored and diced
- Crispy chickpeas
- 1 recipe Spicy Maple Tahini Sauce

INSTRUCTIONS
a) Preheat the oven to 425°F (220°C, or gas mark 7).

b) Add the farro, water, and a generous pinch of salt to a medium saucepan. Bring to a boil, then reduce the heat to low, cover, and simmer until the farro is tender with a slight chew, about 30 minutes.

c) Meanwhile, toss the squash and Brussels sprouts with the oil, salt, and pepper. Spread in a single layer on a rimmed baking sheet. Roast until the squash is tender and the Brussels sprouts are browned and crispy, about 20 minutes, stirring once halfway through.

d) To serve, divide the kale among bowls. Top with squash, Brussels sprouts, farro, radicchio, and apple. Sprinkle with crispy chickpeas and drizzle with Spicy Maple Tahini Sauce.

85. Masala Chickpea Bowls

INGREDIENTS:
- 1 small head cauliflower, cut into florets
- 3 medium carrots, peeled and cut into ¼-inch (6 mm)-thick slices 4 tablespoons (60 ml) avocado or extra-virgin olive oil, divided
- Kosher salt and freshly ground black pepper
- 1 small onion, diced
- 2 cloves garlic, minced
- 1 tablespoon (6 g) finely grated fresh ginger
- 1 small Serrano chile, seeded and diced (optional)
- 2 teaspoons (4 g) garam masala
- 1 teaspoon (2 g) ground coriander
- ½ teaspoon ground turmeric
- 1 (14-ounce, or 392 g) can diced tomatoes
- 1½ cups (300 g) or 1 (15-ounce, or 420 g) can chickpeas, drained and rinsed
- ½ cup (90 g) millet
- 1¼ cups (295 ml) water
- 4 cups (280 g) chopped Swiss chard
- 1 recipe Cilantro Yogurt Sauce

INSTRUCTIONS
a) Preheat the oven to 400°F (200°C, or gas mark 6).
b) Toss the cauliflower and carrots with 2 tablespoons (30 ml) of the oil, salt, and pepper. Spread in an even layer on a rimmed baking sheet. Roast for 20 minutes, stirring once halfway through.
c) Heat 1 tablespoon (15 ml) oil in a large skillet over medium heat. Add the onion, season with salt and pepper, and cook, stirring occasionally, until soft, about 5 minutes. Add the garlic, ginger, Serrano chile (if using), garam masala, coriander, and turmeric, and stir to combine. Cook until fragrant, about 2 minutes. Stir in the tomatoes, chickpeas,

and another pinch of salt and pepper. Bring to a boil, then reduce the heat and simmer for 15 minutes, stirring occasionally. Meanwhile, prepare the millet.

d) Add the millet to a large, dry saucepan and toast over medium heat until golden brown, 4 to 5 minutes. Pour in the water and a generous pinch of salt. The water will sputter at first but will settle quickly. Bring to a boil. Reduce the heat to low, cover, and simmer until most of the water is absorbed, about 15 minutes. Remove from the heat and steam in the pot for 5 minutes.

e) Heat the remaining 1 tablespoon (15 ml) oil in a skillet over medium heat. Add the chard, season lightly with salt and pepper, and toss to coat with the oil. Cook until tender, 3 to 5 minutes.

f) To serve, divide the millet and chard among bowls. Top with chickpeas and tomatoes, roasted cauliflower and carrots.

86. Moroccan-Spiced Chickpea Bowls

INGREDIENTS:

- 3 tablespoons (45 ml) avocado or extra-virgin olive oil, divided
- ½ medium onion, diced
- 2 cloves garlic, minced
- 2 teaspoons (4 g) harissa
- 1 teaspoon (5 g) tomato paste
- 2 teaspoons (4 g) ground cumin
- 1 teaspoon (2 g) paprika
- ½ teaspoon ground cinnamon
- Kosher salt and freshly ground black pepper
- 2 cups (400 g) chickpeas, drained
- 1 (14-ounce, or 392 g) can diced tomatoes
- ¾ cup (125 g) bulgur
- 1½ cups (355 ml) water
- 8 packed cups (560 g) shredded kale
- 2 avocados, peeled, pitted, and thinly sliced
- 4 poached eggs
- 1 recipe Mint Yogurt Sauce

INSTRUCTIONS

a) Heat 2 tablespoons (30 ml) of the oil in a skillet over medium heat until shimmering. Add the onion and cook, stirring occasionally, until soft and fragrant, about 5 minutes. Stir in the garlic, harissa, tomato paste, cumin, paprika, cinnamon, salt, and pepper, and cook for 2 minutes. Stir in the chickpeas and tomatoes. Bring to a boil, then reduce the heat to low and simmer for 20 minutes. Meanwhile, prepare the bulgur.

b) Combine the bulgur, water, and a generous pinch of salt in a medium saucepan. Bring to a boil. Reduce the heat to low, cover, and simmer until tender, 10 to 15 minutes.

c) Heat the remaining 1 tablespoon (15 ml) oil in a skillet over medium heat until shimmering. Add the kale and season with salt. Cook, stirring occasionally, until soft and wilted, about 5 minutes.

d) To serve, divide the bulgur among bowls. Top with chickpeas and tomatoes, kale, avocado, and an egg. Drizzle with Mint Yogurt Sauce.

87. Beet Falafel Bowls

INGREDIENTS:

- 3 cups (600 g) or 2 (15-ounce, or 420 g) cans chickpeas, drained and rinsed
- 1 small red onion, roughly chopped
- ½ packed cup (24 g) fresh parsley leaves
- ½ packed cup (24 g) fresh cilantro leaves
- 2 tablespoons (30 ml) freshly squeezed lemon juice
- 2 cloves garlic
- 2 teaspoons (4 g) ground cumin
- 1 teaspoon (2 g) ground coriander
- $1/8$ teaspoon cayenne pepper
- Kosher salt and freshly ground black pepper
- 3 tablespoons (24 g) all-purpose flour
- 1 teaspoon (2 g) baking powder
- 8 (5-inch, or 13 cm) baby carrots, with stems still attached
- 1 tablespoon (15 ml) avocado or extra-virgin olive oil
- 16 ounces (455 g) spiralized beet noodles
- 2 packed cups (140 g) finely shredded
- Tuscan kale
- ½ English cucumber, chopped
- 1 recipe Avocado Green Goddess
- Dressing

INSTRUCTIONS

a) If using dried beans, add the chickpeas to a medium bowl and cover with water by at least 1 inch (2.5 cm). Let them sit, uncovered, at room temperature for 24 hours.

b) Preheat the oven to 375°F (190°C, or gas mark 5).

c) Add the drained chickpeas, onion, parsley, cilantro, lemon juice, garlic, cumin, coriander, cayenne, 1 teaspoon (6 g) salt, and ¼ teaspoon pepper to the bowl of a food processor. Pulse about 10 times until the chickpeas are chopped. Scrape down the sides of the bowl, add the flour and baking powder, and pulse until the mixture is well combined.

d) Scoop out about 2 tablespoons (30 g) of the mixture and roll it into a ball in the palms of your hands. Transfer to a lightly greased baking sheet and use a spatula to flatten into a $\frac{1}{2}$-inch (1.3 cm)-thick disk. Repeat with the remainder of the mixture.

e) Bake the falafel until cooked through and tender, 25 to 30 minutes, flipping once halfway through.

f) Cut the carrots in half lengthwise. Toss with the oil, salt, and pepper, and arrange in a single layer on a rimmed baking sheet. Cook until tender, about 20 minutes.

g) To serve, divide the beet noodles and kale among bowls. Top with falafel patties, roasted carrots, and cucumber, and drizzle with Avocado Green Goddess Dressing.

88. Harissa Chicken Bowls

INGREDIENTS:
- 1 pound (455 g) boneless, skinless chicken breast, cut into 1-inch
- (2.5 cm) cubes
- 1 teaspoon (2 g) ground cumin
- 1 teaspoon (2 g) ground coriander
- ½ teaspoon ground cardamom
- Kosher salt and freshly ground black pepper
- 2 medium zucchini, sliced into ½-inch (1.3 cm)-thick rounds
- 3 tablespoons (45 ml) avocado or extra-virgin olive oil, divided
- ¾ cup (125 g) cracked freekeh
- 2 cups (470 ml) water
- 1 tablespoon (6 g) plus 1 teaspoon
- (2 g) harissa, divided
- 2 cups (300 g) cherry tomatoes
- ½ cup (120 ml) chicken stock
- 2 cups (140 g) chopped Swiss chard 1 medium bulb fennel, trimmed and thinly sliced
- 1½ cups (300 g) or 1 (15-ounce, or 420 g) can chickpeas, drained and rinsed
- 1 recipe Creamy Mint Feta Sauce

INSTRUCTIONS

a) Preheat the oven to 400°F (200°C, or gas mark 6).

b) 2 Add the chicken to a large bowl along with the cumin, coriander, cardamom, salt, and pepper. Toss until the chicken is well coated; set aside while you prep the vegetables and freekeh.

c) Toss the zucchini with 1 tablespoon (15 ml) of the oil, salt, and pepper. Spread in a single layer on a rimmed baking sheet. Roast for 20 minutes, flipping halfway through.

d) Meanwhile, combine the freekeh, water, and a generous pinch of salt in a medium saucepan. Bring to a boil, then reduce the heat to low, cover, and simmer for 15 minutes, stirring occasionally, until all the liquid has been absorbed and the freekeh is tender. Remove from the heat and stir in 1 tablespoon (15 ml) of oil and 1 teaspoon (2 g) of the harissa.

e) Heat the remaining 1 tablespoon (15 ml) oil in a large skillet over high heat until very hot but not smoking. Add the chicken and sear on all sides, 1 to 2 minutes per side. Stir in the tomatoes and cook just until they begin to pop, about 2 minutes. Add the remaining 1 tablespoon (6 g) harissa and chicken stock, and stir to combine. Bring to a boil, then reduce the heat to low, and simmer for 3 minutes.

f) To serve, divide the freekeh and Swiss chard among bowls. Top with chicken and tomatoes, roasted zucchini, fennel, and chickpeas.

g) Drizzle with Creamy Mint Feta Sauce.

89. Greek Power Bowls

INGREDIENTS:
- 1 cup (165 g) bulgur
- 2 cups (470 ml) water
- Kosher salt and freshly ground black pepper
- 1 tablespoon (15 ml) avocado or extra-virgin olive oil
- ½ medium red onion, diced
- 1 clove garlic, minced
- ½ pound (228 g) ground lamb
- 1 teaspoon (1 g) dried oregano
- 1 teaspoon (2 g) ground coriander
- ½ teaspoon paprika
- 1 cup (200 g) chickpeas, drained and rinsed
- 3 cups (165 g) chopped romaine or mixed greens
- ½ English cucumber, halved and sliced
- 2 plum tomatoes, chopped
- ½ cup (50 g) pitted kalamata olives
- Hummus
- 1 recipe Creamy Feta Sauce

INSTRUCTIONS

a) Combine the bulgur, water, and a pinch of salt in a medium saucepan. Bring to a boil, then reduce the heat to low, cover, and simmer until tender and all the water has been absorbed, 10 to 15 minutes.

b) Heat the oil in a medium skillet over medium heat. Add the onion and garlic, and sauté until soft, about 3 minutes. Add the lamb, season with salt and pepper, and cook, breaking up the meat with a wooden spoon, until browned and cooked through, 6 to 8 minutes. Stir in the oregano, coriander, paprika, and chickpeas, and cook, stirring occasionally, until the spices are fragrant and the chickpeas are heated through, about 3 minutes.

c) To serve, divide the bulgur among bowls. Top with the lamb and chickpea mixture, lettuce, cucumber, tomato, olives, hummus, and Creamy Feta Sauce.

DESSERT

90. Chickpea choco slices

INGREDIENTS:
- 400 g can chickpeas, rinsed, drained.
- 250 g almond butter.
- 70 ml maple syrup.
- 15 ml vanilla paste.
- 1 pinch salt.
- 2 g baking powder.
- 2 g baking soda.
- 40 g vegan chocolate chips.

INSTRUCTIONS:
a) Preheat oven to 180° C/350° F.
b) Grease large baking pan with coconut oil.
c) Combine chickpeas, almond butter, maple syrup, vanilla, salt, baking powder, and baking soda in a food blender.
d) Blend until smooth. Stir in half the chocolate chips spread the batter into the prepared baking pan.
e) Sprinkle with reserved chocolate chips.
f) Bake for 45-50 minutes or until an inserted toothpick comes out clean.
g) Cool on a wire rack for 20 minutes. Slice and serve.

91. Chickpea Chocolate Chip Cookies

INGREDIENTS:
- 1 can (15 oz) chickpeas, drained and rinsed
- 1/2 cup almond butter
- 1/4 cup maple syrup
- 1 teaspoon vanilla extract
- 1/2 teaspoon baking powder
- 1/4 teaspoon salt
- 1/2 cup chocolate chips

INSTRUCTIONS:
a) Preheat the oven to 350°F (175°C).
b) In a food processor, blend the chickpeas, almond butter, maple syrup, vanilla extract, baking powder, and salt until smooth.
c) Stir in the chocolate chips.
d) Drop spoonfuls of the dough onto a baking sheet lined with parchment paper.
e) Bake for 12-15 minutes or until the edges are golden brown.
f) Allow the cookies to cool before serving.

92. Chickpea Blondies

INGREDIENTS:

- 1 can (15 oz) chickpeas, drained and rinsed
- 1/2 cup almond butter
- 1/3 cup maple syrup
- 2 teaspoons vanilla extract
- 1/2 teaspoon baking powder
- 1/4 teaspoon salt
- 1/2 cup chocolate chips

INSTRUCTIONS:

a) Preheat the oven to 350°F (175°C).
b) In a food processor, blend the chickpeas, almond butter, maple syrup, vanilla extract, baking powder, and salt until smooth.
c) Stir in the chocolate chips.
d) Pour the batter into a greased baking dish.
e) Bake for 20-25 minutes or until the edges are golden brown and a toothpick inserted into the center comes out clean.
f) Allow the blondies to cool before cutting into squares.

93. Chickpea Chocolate Mousse

INGREDIENTS:
- 1 can (15 oz) chickpeas, drained and rinsed
- 1/4 cup cocoa powder
- 1/4 cup maple syrup
- 1 teaspoon vanilla extract
- Pinch of salt
- Optional toppings: whipped coconut cream, fresh berries, chopped nuts

INSTRUCTIONS:
a) In a food processor, blend the chickpeas, cocoa powder, maple syrup, vanilla extract, and salt until smooth.
b) Transfer the mixture to serving glasses or bowls.
c) Refrigerate for at least 2 hours to set.
d) Top with whipped coconut cream, fresh berries, or chopped nuts before serving.

94. Chickpea Peanut Butter Cups

INGREDIENTS:
- 1 can (15 oz) chickpeas, drained and rinsed
- 1/4 cup peanut butter
- 2 tablespoons maple syrup
- 1/4 cup coconut oil, melted
- 1/4 cup cocoa powder
- 1 teaspoon vanilla extract
- Pinch of salt

INSTRUCTIONS:
a) In a food processor, blend the chickpeas, peanut butter, maple syrup, coconut oil, cocoa powder, vanilla extract, and salt until smooth.
b) Line a muffin tin with paper liners.
c) Spoon a small amount of the mixture into the bottom of each muffin cup, spreading it evenly.
d) Place the muffin tin in the freezer for 10 minutes to firm up the bottom layer.
e) Remove the muffin tin from the freezer and spoon the remaining mixture over the bottom layer, covering it completely.
f) Return the muffin tin to the freezer for 1-2 hours to set.
g) Once set, remove the peanut butter cups from the muffin tin and store them in an airtight container in the refrigerator.

95. Chickpea Brownies

INGREDIENTS:
- 1 can (15 oz) chickpeas, drained and rinsed
- 1/2 cup almond butter
- 1/3 cup maple syrup
- 1/4 cup cocoa powder
- 1 teaspoon vanilla extract
- 1/2 teaspoon baking powder
- 1/4 teaspoon salt
- 1/2 cup chocolate chips

INSTRUCTIONS:
a) Preheat the oven to 350°F (175°C).
b) In a food processor, blend the chickpeas, almond butter, maple syrup, cocoa powder, vanilla extract, baking powder, and salt until smooth.
c) Stir in the chocolate chips.
d) Pour the batter into a greased baking dish.
e) Bake for 25-30 minutes or until a toothpick inserted into the center comes out with a few moist crumbs.
f) Allow the brownies to cool before cutting into squares.

96. Chickpea Coconut Macaroons

INGREDIENTS:
- 1 can (15 oz) chickpeas, drained and rinsed
- 1/2 cup shredded coconut
- 1/4 cup maple syrup
- 1 teaspoon vanilla extract
- Pinch of salt
- Optional: melted chocolate for drizzling

INSTRUCTIONS:
a) Preheat the oven to 350°F (175°C).
b) In a food processor, blend the chickpeas, shredded coconut, maple syrup, vanilla extract, and salt until smooth.
c) Scoop tablespoon-sized portions of the mixture onto a baking sheet lined with parchment paper.
d) Use your fingers to shape the portions into small mounds.
e) Bake for 15-18 minutes or until the edges are golden brown.
f) Allow the macaroons to cool before drizzling with melted chocolate, if desired.

97. Chickpea Pumpkin Pie Bars

INGREDIENTS:
- 1 can (15 oz) chickpeas, drained and rinsed
- 1 cup pumpkin puree
- 1/4 cup maple syrup
- 1/4 cup coconut flour
- 1/4 cup almond milk
- 2 teaspoons pumpkin pie spice
- 1 teaspoon vanilla extract
- Pinch of salt
- Optional toppings: whipped coconut cream, cinnamon

INSTRUCTIONS:
a) Preheat the oven to 350°F (175°C).
b) In a food processor, blend the chickpeas, pumpkin puree, maple syrup, coconut flour, almond milk, pumpkin pie spice, vanilla extract, and salt until smooth.
c) Pour the batter into a greased baking dish.
d) Bake for 25-30 minutes or until the center is set.
e) Allow the bars to cool before cutting into squares.
f) Serve with whipped coconut cream and a sprinkle of cinnamon, if desired.

DRINKS

98. Blackberry Marshmallow Cream Soda

INGREDIENTS:
- 1 shot of Blackberry Simple Syrup
- 1 shot of Gin
- Soda Water
- 1 big dollop of Marshmallow Fluff

MARSHMALLOW FLUFF
- 1 10 ounces bag of Dandies Mini Marshmallows
- Liquid from 1 can of Chickpeas
- 1 teaspoon Coconut Oil

INSTRUCTIONS:
a) Fill a glass with ice. Pour in 1 shot of blackberry simple syrup and a shot of gin, and stir. Fill the rest of the way with soda and top with a dollop of marshmallow fluff.

MARSHMALLOW FLUFF
b) In a stand mixer whip aquafaba until fluffy peaks form in the meringue. Meanwhile, in a microwave-safe bowl combine coconut oil and marshmallows. In 30-second intervals, giving a quick stir between each, microwave until the marshmallows have fully melted.

c) Add the marshmallow mixture into the stand mixer with the meringue and whip together until smooth.

d) Store in an air-tight container in the fridge for up to 5 days.

99. Butterfly Pea Dalgona coffee

INGREDIENTS:
- 2 tablespoons sugar
- 2 tablespoons boiling water
- Liquid from a can of chickpeas/aquafaba
- 1 teaspoon butterfly pea powder
- 2 cups oat milk

INSTRUCTIONS:

a) Strain a can of chickpeas into a bowl to use the liquid from the can.
b) Use a handheld electric mixer to whip them until fluffy.
c) Meanwhile, boil water and pour two tablespoons into a bowl with sugar and butterfly pea powder to dissolve. Once the aquafaba is frothy, add in the blue bowl of sugary goodness.
d) Whip until frothy! Be patient.
e) Fill two mini small jars with oat milk and ice and spoon the frothy blue on top.
f) Garnish with some edible flowers.

100. Aquafaba Whipped Coffee

INGREDIENTS:
- 2 tablespoons instant coffee
- 2 tablespoons sugar
- 2 tablespoons hot water
- 4 tablespoons aquafaba (chickpea brine)
- Ice cubes
- Milk of your choice (regular, almond, oat, etc.)

INSTRUCTIONS:
a) In a medium-sized bowl, combine instant coffee, sugar, and hot water.
b) Using an electric mixer or whisk, beat the aquafaba in a separate bowl until it becomes frothy and starts to form stiff peaks, similar to whipped cream.
c) Gently fold the coffee mixture into the whipped aquafaba until well combined.
d) Fill a glass with ice cubes and pour milk over the ice.
e) Spoon the whipped coffee mixture on top of the milk.
f) Stir gently to combine the coffee with the milk before drinking.
g) Sip and enjoy your delicious and fluffy aquafaba whipped coffee!

CONCLUSION

As our chickpea-inspired adventure comes to a close, we hope this cookbook has inspired you to embrace the remarkable versatility of this superfood and explore its limitless potential in your own kitchen. Chickpeas have proven to be an invaluable ingredient, adding both nutrition and flavor to countless dishes.

We encourage you to continue experimenting with chickpeas, adapting the recipes in this cookbook to suit your tastes and preferences. Whether you're adding them to soups, stews, salads, or even baking them into decadent treats, chickpeas have the power to transform ordinary dishes into extraordinary culinary experiences.

We hope this cookbook has provided you with a newfound appreciation for chickpeas and their ability to nourish both body and soul. Share your creations with loved ones, celebrate the joys of wholesome and delicious cooking, and revel in the knowledge that you're not only enhancing your own well-being but also making a positive impact on the planet.

Thank you for joining us on this chickpea-filled journey. May your kitchen always be filled with the aroma of delightful spices and the satisfaction of wholesome meals. Happy cooking and bon appétit!

www.ingramcontent.com/pod-product-compliance
Lightning Source LLC
LaVergne TN
LVHW021658060526
838200LV00050B/2406